Look the Part to Get the Role

Look the Part
to
Get the Role

40 **Days to Looking, Branding, and Becoming the Role You Want to Play in Your Life**

The Ultimate Visual Branding Guide

BRANDI MITCHELL

Visual Brand Strategist & Image Coach

KORIS PUBLISHING

This book includes information gathered from many personal experiences. It is published for general reference and is not intended to be a substitute for independent verification by readers when necessary and appropriate. The book is sold with the understanding that neither the author nor publisher is engaged in rendering legal, or psychological advice. The publisher and author disclaim any personal liability, directly or indirectly, for advice or information presented within. Although the author and publisher have prepared this manuscript with utmost care and diligence and have made every effort to ensure the accuracy and completeness of the information contained within, we assume no responsibility for errors, inaccuracies, omissions or inconsistencies.

Look the Part to Get the Role

ISBN – 978-0-9885299-0-8
Copyright 2013 by Brandi Mitchell
Published by Koris Publishing LLC
Roswell, Georgia 30076

Printed in the United States of America.
All rights reserved under International Copyright Law.

Cover by Carolyn Sheltraw
Cover photo by Allen Cooley
Author Photo by Corey Cotrell

Quantity discounts are available to your company, educational institution, or church

For reselling, educational purposes, counseling groups, subscription incentives, gifts, or fundraising campaigns

For more information, please contact the publisher at
admin@looktheparttogettherole.com

Visit us on the web!
www.looktheparttogettherole.com

To My Four Guys
My husband Curtis, my supporter, best friend, and the love of my life.
Kory, who brings us unimaginable joy,
And Brannen & Curtis for their sweet spirits.

To my parents Shirley & Don Hennings
And my Grandparents Annie & Robert Morris
who loved and cared for me unselfishly
to make me the woman which became the wife of Curtis,
and mother of Kory, Brannen, and Curtis.
May your dreams be realized through me.

And to the Director of my Life, My Lord and Savior Jesus Christ

ACKNOWLEDGEMENTS

I am so absolutely grateful for being able to live out my dreams and by doing so – inspire and empower women and men to present their very best image, and explore their own God-given dreams. My journey from psychology major, to celebrity makeup and hair stylist, to entrepreneur, and director has been a divine assignment that I have been escorted on with very special people.

Endless thank you's go to the team that worked on this book, Carolyn Sheltraw, Allen Cooley, Shirley Hennings, and Tunda Wannamaker, for pushing and praying me across the finish line.

To my husband and best friend Curtis, from the day I met you, you have always remained to be a kind, supportive, and joy to call husband. You dream just as hard as I do, and together we get to experience the world through the same eyes. Thank you for always listening, and having an open heart to help me pursue every dream I've ever had. Your strength, love, and kindness strengthen me and show not only me, but our family and all those you encounter, how we should model Christ's love.

To Kory, you bring me so much joy just watching you develop as a young man of excellence. Continue to march to your own drum, pursue your gifts, and keep that loving heart. You will inspire many with your life. To

Brannen and Curtis, thank you for allowing me to speak into your lives, continue to carve out paths of your own, knowing that you can truly have a life you love if you put in the work and make good choices.

To my Mom, you taught me by example, that beauty, style, and grace are great, but secondary to kindness and integrity. You taught me that the most beautiful person is not measured by what's outside, but what's inside. I always remember you reminding me of what was important growing up by saying " People can always change their appearance on the outside, so always look at the character of a person, because it's hard changing an ugly heart". Thank you for your encouragement, strength, and unending love.

To my Father, who was never without a camera in his hand to capture all of life's moments, and who took me on my very first photoshoot – I love you. You didn't realize the seeds you were planting as you lived your life full out in front of me, but your influence will forever be present in all that I do. You showed me what was possible, opened up my world to endless possibilities, and helped to fuel and fund my dreams. I pray that you would be proud of the paths I've chosen.

To my Grandparents who are both passed on but live on within me. Thank you for loving me, supporting me, and for every goody bag you sent me home with every time I visited your house! My heart remains warm when I think about my childhood because of your presence and influence.

To the Mitchell and Early Family thank you for your support, love, acceptance, and kindness throughout the years.

To a man who was a quiet giant to me who has transitioned on; Uncle Jimmy.

To my Uncle Marc for allowing me to first understand and get exposed to artist development through endless moments of listening to your songs on cold Michigan days in your car. Thank you for trusting my opinion and helping me to develop my branding muscle with every song, performance, and photo shoot. Thank you for allowing me to share in all of your trips all over the world, and paving the way for me to see a bright future.

To my brother Jason, I love the fact that in our forties we are getting to truly get to know each other greater, and realize that we are so much alike. I love you.

Pastors Mirek & Linda Hufton and Pastors Reginald & Kelly Lane for guiding me towards, and unearthing my spiritual DNA.

To DeVon Franklin, thank you for being an excellent model of pursuing your dream boldy without compromise. Thank you for your inspirational words and unconscious mentorship you have provided in the support of this book. I am so glad our paths crossed, and I look forward to the future.

To all those who contributed to my growth as an artist and entrepreneur: Carmen McCloud, John Atchison, John Gooden, Jacqueline Robinson, Meagan Mitchell, Sanya Weston, Carlene & Mitchell Jones, Lexi Allen, Renee Wallace, Waleed Shamsid-Deen, Nicole Slyvester, Simmons-Shelley, Campeau Advertising, Motivating the Masses, Preston Whitmore, Toni Judkins, TV One, Michael Baisden, Ameen Howrani, and Steve Harvey.

To my wonderful clients I have been able to service throughout the years by ushering them to their next level – I am grateful that you choose me!

To God, a friend, father, and director like no other. Thank you for showing me your goodness while in my valleys and in the mountains; teaching me how to trust you in either.

TABLE OF CONTENTS

Act One: Discovery and Defining the Role You Want

Realize That Every Day You Are Auditioning

You, The Celebrity Of Your Business and Life

What's Your Role? Know it. Study It. Play It Well.

Get Rid of the Negative Inner Chatter So You Don't Sabotage Your Big Break!

Act Two: How to Look the Part

You Are Here. What's Your Before?

Act Three: Getting & Owning Your Role

INTRODUCTION

While growing up, I spent several Saturdays at my Grandmother's home in Detroit. Being an only child, my favorite past times were eating fresh plums from her plum tree and tomatoes from her garden, listening to her stellar collection of Earth, Wind & Fire, Peabo Bryson, Stevie Wonder, Michael Jackson, and Donna Summers records, looking at countless photo albums of immaculately styled pictures of my family, rummaging her beautiful clothing and makeup, and daily lessons in the way of the Motown Inspired/Old Hollywood Glamour and charm. I naturally inherited the love for "looking the part" from my Mother and Grandmother who not only taught me how to present myself for where I want to go; but also emphasized being grateful for where I have been. As I relentlessly studied my grandmothers beautiful pictures taken from nights out with my Grandfather and my Aunts at an old Detroit staple called the 20 Grand Club, it was as if I stepped back in time to the glory days of Motown – complete with flawless hair, makeup, and beautiful gowns.

My grandmother kept every piece of clothing from those days; and I spent from sun up to sun down recreating the outfits that I saw her wear in those photo albums. I was the first grandchild and my Mothers only child, so I grew to be extremely creative, and found countless ways of amusing myself. I would recreate scenes in my head through my grandmothers pictures and clothing of Marvin Gaye singing to Tami Terrell,

The Temptations dancing in unison, and the Supremes serenading the crowd.

What I learned from my mother and grandmother was the skill of putting together a head-to-toe polished look – something they did as a daily standard in observance of the day and time they lived in -The Golden days of Motown Records. Their way of life and fashion norm was making a statement with their clothing and their appearance - presenting a look that was somehow regal.

By the age of 7, I performed my first "weave" when I realized I could cut the hair off of one dolls hair and sew it to the other doll's hair who I felt needed more hair. I began taking hand me down clothing from my family members and redesigning it to meet the current days fashion by the age of 11, by age 13 I pierced my own ears with ice and a needle, at sixteen I made my own sweet sixteen dress, and by 17, after being inspired by the Salt n Pepa "Shoop" video, I gave myself their signature asymmetrical cut. Out of necessity, I learned how to be extremely savvy with taking one outfit and making it look multiple ways through accessories. By the time I arrived at college I supported myself by doing hair in the dorms; I quickly learned that I could make triple the amount of money doing something I enjoyed rather than working at a fast food joint.

My major in college was psychology. I decided to pursue psychology because I wanted to truly help my grandmother. The same grandmother that introduced me to class and charm, and had a heart of gold. My grandmother often visited psychiatrists, and after experiencing years of seeing her go to the psychiatrists to simply "be heard", it appeared that they never provided solutions – to me, nothing changed.

2

To look at my grandmother, even at age 70, you could still see that she was cut from a different cloth. A woman of Sicilian, Cherokee Indian, and African American descent, she had a class and presence that would rival any Hollywood starlet – but appeared to be trapped. My grandmother, in her hay day was so absolutely stunning that she could walk down the street and literally cause accidents. Grandma's childhood got cut short when she got married at 16, and suddenly found herself not only a wife but also a mother.

What I believe could have been a tremendous turning point in her life was when she was approached by a casting director to play a role in a soft drinks national commercial. Should she have accepted, she would have been the first woman of color to ever be in this national campaign. Excited, she ran home to tell my grandfather, only for him to forbid her to do the commercial. What could have been the start of a new career got canceled by one word - no.

My grandmother would go on to raise her family, always adorned in beautiful clothes and looking like she stepped out of a magazine. But the frustration of her life, I truly believe, was not being able to explore the "what's possible" in her life.

What could have been possible if she had done that commercial? If she had truly pursued her dreams?

My grandmother's common saying was actually the motivation for this book. She would say "If you can't look the part, don't play the role". Grandma absolutely look the part, but I truly think her dismay was that she didn't fully live out what was possible, and get the role she was born to play.

Every one tells me that I have the personality of my grandmother; even she thought so. After seeing her life, it made me determined to explore the "what's possible" in life. I was determined to enjoy looking the part, but also get the role.

This saying became somewhat a theme in my life both personally and professionally. As I reflect back on my 20 plus years working in the beauty industry as a celebrity makeup and hair artist, and now owning a consulting and training company; my Grandma's life, presence, and her lessons are woven throughout what I do and how and *why* I consult.

I learned, while grooming and maintaining the brands of celebrities, that we truly have the ability to create our own realities. We have the ability to shape how we are viewed, and since image is king, we can brand ourselves to represent our roles, and sell the product of ourselves to accelerate or solidify the impression we want to make on the world.

LOOK THE PART TO GET THE ROLE is the essence of what I experienced through years of working in television and film; adapted to benefit every day people in a way that propels them to become the celebrities of their own life.

LOOK THE PART TO GET THE ROLE is not another makeover book, nor is it a branding book alone. Look the Part to Get the Role connects your purpose to your image, deals with things that would cause roadblocks, and empowers you to stand unapologetically in your greatness. This book will allow you to see yourself as the celebrity of your own life, and equips you with the tools to tell your story through your image in such a way that you are undeniable.

LOOK THE PART TO GET THE ROLE will challenge you to truly look at where you are playing small, refocus you in the direction of what you really want, and show you how to look fabulous doing it all.

LOOK THE PART TO GET THE ROLE is about helping you get the guts to explore the "what's possible" in your own life and image. It's about making you awaken and demonstrate to the world and yourself the star within.

Every day I see people living at only a fraction of what truly is possible. They too are trapped either in low self esteem, following monotony, or fear. The frustration of knowing that there is more to achieve in life, and not quite knowing how to get there, is riveting.

But it doesn't have to be your story; you can choose to tell another story – today.

With this book, I celebrate my Grandmother. I celebrate her by empowering others to know they can play out their roles in life, and look awesome doing so. In her own way, she inspired me to boldly explore the "what's possible" in my own life. Somehow I have to think that she lives on in me, and the dreams she had are being actualized through my life – and now yours.

Day 1

Every Day Is An Audition

Audition: An audition is a test at
which a performer or musician is
asked to demonstrate their ability
for a particular role.

Ask any successful actor and they will tell you they went on more auditions than they can remember. In fact, many actors will hear "no" more than they will hear "yes". But, ah, to receive that one yes makes all the no's worth it! The ultimate goal of any actor or performer is to go in to every audition to get the role. Most actors, even those seasoned performers, still have to audition to get the roles they want to further their career. All aspiring actors know the right role could catapult their career taking them from waiting tables to super stardom in a matter of a few minutes of screen time.

Auditioning usually consists of an actor studying for a particular role in a production, and the actor gets cast in the role based on how much they literally become the character. The actor has to go before one person or a group of decision-makers, ranging from a casting agent to the director, who then decide if the actor fits the part and can embody the character in the production.

And just as actors can get their big break by landing the role of a lifetime, you can get your big break in the role you play on your job, in your business and on your own personal stage of life. It all starts with how prepared you are to get the role you want.

You see every time we get dressed and walk out the door to go to a meeting, every time we're running errands or we meet with a potential client, each time we attend a networking event, or we speak before our peers, we are literally auditioning. Believe it or not, even when you're going to your child's school or meeting some of your husband's co-workers, you are deciding your own fate - casting yourself in the role of your choice.

Whether you get the role will be based on how well you decide to show up and represent your role; in other words, it will depend on how well you look the part. Some people, who are oblivious to how much image impacts what they do will say that I'm going a little bit overboard with my analogy of auditioning. But having been in the entertainment industry for over 20 years, and having groomed celebrities, media professionals, and actors who in fact have the roles, I have an insider point of view of the auditioning process. And I have to tell you that what the actors go through and what you everyday celebrities have to go through to get your roles in life are one in the same.

I know the importance of first impressions, and how it literally can be the thing to get you in the door, and provide opportunities for you. Whether you make the right impression to those important decision-makers in your life boils down to how well you prepare to win for every audition you pursue.

So every day when you go out, and present yourself to the world, the best thing you can ever do is treat every day as if it's an audition. Treat every day as if it could be a big break to elevate you to expose you to something magnificent. Just think about how many opportunities may present themselves to you while you're in the grocery store, while you're in line at the post office, while you're in a meeting, or even in the carpool lane. Every time you interact with someone, you have an opportunity to audition for yet another role, or a role that's going to help you further what it is that you really want to accomplish. The cool thing is, you can position yourself to get any role you want! How exciting!

I have been very fortunate to have very divinely orchestrated opportunities present themselves in ways that seem unimaginable for some. I always tell people that when opportunity knocked, it would not find me unprepared to seize it. Being prepared is the true element for success; being fabulous when it finds you seals the deal! I always look at each and every experience as an opportunity for something great to happen. And because I have that perspective, when I show up to seize an opportunity, I decide what I want to convey to the world through my image and presence. I'm showing up, and I'm saying:

"Yes, I am a CEO"

"Yes I am a visual brand strategist"

"Yes I can be someone that you can trust to help you with your image"

"Yes, I can help you tell your story"

When I present myself, everything I do in terms of my image should be purposed to give off an impression of credibility. It solidifies a level of trust when I say I am someone that will be able to help you in your journey – all while I am auditioning for you. I am also aware and have prepared myself through research to already know the script of those I am auditioning for, so I know who they are and am familiar with their expectations. Through studying for the role I want, I bring who I am, and tweak it to fit their culture all while staying consistent with my brand. This can only be achieved when you know and have clarity about who you are. The treasure of who you are is what I hope to help you unlock during this 40-day experience.

So today I want you to be honest with yourself. Would you ace your audition?

Based off of what you are projecting when you go out a day-to-day basis, if someone were going to give you an opportunity, would that person give you an opportunity based on how you present yourself? Or would you need to convince that person by what it is you say, by showing your intellect, by showing your credentials, or by talking about who you know or what you've done? I want you to take a good look over the next 40 days, and make a log of what you wear every day. Then I want you to ask yourself very important questions. Are you listening? Would you cast yourself in your role? I want you to be honest and ask yourself, if you saw yourself, would you be someone that you would want to play with - meaning, someone that you will want to do business with and someone you will want to get to know?

If the answer is no, then begin to ask yourself, why?

Actors who are successful with the audition process are the ones who come prepared. Actors who do well on auditions know exactly what is expected of them, these actors come looking the part and allow the character's personality to shine through to prove themselves worthy of getting the part.

Allow your image to cast you in the roles that you want in your life. Look at every day, every event, every conversation, as a potential audition. Determine for yourself that you will put every effort to show up to the audition prepared to get the role.

Day 2

The 50% Director's Rule, and How I Used It To Get My First Big Break

Big Break: An event that changes life in a positive way; something that will open up more opportunities in the future; an accomplishment that will lead to more accomplishments; something that causes a distinctive change either in one's career or personal life

The fate and career of an aspiring actor can be determined by a single role, a role that is usually awarded by a casting director, or the actual director of the project. When directors cast roles, there is an unspoken rule that is not only true in Hollywood, but also applicable for we "every day celebrities". Every day celebrities are those that I believe are performing every day on their own stages of life, just not with the cameras following them! This rule is called the 50% Director's Rule. The 50% Director's Rule is this books methodology in a nutshell. It also encompasses my three-part process that is essential to every great visual brand, which is "Look the Part, Get The Role, and Own it."

Part One: Look the part. The 50% Directors rule is simple; it means that in an audition, 50% of any role is cast when an actor enters the room! He (or she) doesn't have to say one word – they just LOOK like the character, literally they ARE the character when they come in the room.

Part Two: Have the ability to get the role. If the actor actually looks the part of the role, then the next step is to see if they can actually act. The director is looking to see if the actor has the skill, tenacity, and range to embody the role of which they are setting out to win.

Part Three: Authentically own the role. The third component is to see if the actor is believable, authentic, and true to the character's personality. A good performance only happens when both the inner and outer representation of the character is portrayed. For every day celebrities it also means an inner belief that you deserve the role which you seek to obtain or are occupying.

The 50 % Directors Rule is the same in our personal lives, businesses, and in our relationships. Your perception, image, and presentation of the brand of you are doing the heavy lifting when deciding if you win the role.

I used the very same 50% Directors Rules to get my very first break some 13 years ago, a day which changed the trajectory of my life!

I had just finished working on my first independent film in which I was the head of the department – actually I was the entire department. My role: hairstylist, makeup artist, and barber. It was a non-paying job, but the lessons were invaluable. In the beginning of your career as an artist you do a lot of non-paying jobs for exposure and experience. The great thing was this non-paying job led to a paying job. At the end of the film one of the actors wanted me to help with their image for an important audition. In our conversation, they told me of a photographer they thought would really be a fit for me by the name of Ameen Howrani. As a makeup and hairstylist one of the ways that you can really catapult your career is if you work with a great photographer; and Ameen was one of the greats.

Ameen was known for having the ability to capture the powerful faces of every day people in a compelling way and had a magnetic charisma and genuine love for people. From celebrities to large advertising campaigns, Ameen had done it all. A photographer of that stature is very careful of who he brings on his team, because he knows the talent of the individual he hires effects the overall presentation of the finished product to his client. At the end of the day, great photographers want to work with great artists.

To work with Ameen I had to be on my A game and have a portfolio that would reflect the caliber of work worthy of working with him. Working with Ameen would call me to another level in my profession. Ameen did a lot of ad work and photographed the coveted jobs that a makeup and hairstylist does at the height of their career.

Clearly, I was being ballsy in my intent to work with him.

I found myself in a bit of a catch 22. As a freelance makeup and hairstylist, the way you get jobs is basically from the tear sheets that you generate from work you do in editorial campaigns, advertising, and working with celebrities. Each tear sheet can lead you to your next job.

The thing is you need the tear sheets to get the job, and you need the job to get the tear sheet.

To work with Ameen, I had to have a portfolio to even get in the door, but I didn't have the type of photography that truly showcased my work. I had the skill, but not the pictures, which presented a dilemma. You can have all the skill in the world, but a photographer is going to want to know if your work will transfer on film brilliantly, and if you can connect with the vision of the client.

I had three goals to achieve before I could call Ameen to ask for an interview: First I had to bring together a team to create photographs that I could pitch to the photographer to demonstrate my work. Secondly, I had to study to understand the advertising campaign jobs in terms of lighting, hair placement, and products to use. Lastly, what this new and elevated role I wanted looked like physically. I wanted to leave nothing to chance when I walked into the interview. I knew I was the underdog because of the caliber of people the photographer worked with in the past, but I also felt in my gut that if given the chance, I could do it.

After doing all of the prep work, I got the nerve to call for the interview and was granted an interview immediately that same week. This was before people could Google you while talking with you on the phone and immediately see your work or your website. You simply had to sell yourself over the telephone. Let's just say I had practiced my pitch!

The night before the interview with Ameen I could barely sleep. I packed every material I needed just in case he asked me to do any kind of impromptu demo. Being fresh out of college and having decided to forego graduate school for beauty school, I had a lot riding on this interview. I did a great deal of research to find out everything it took to be a successful media makeup and hair artist – I studied for the role I wanted to get. The last component, which was a very important component, was I literally looked like an artist. When I went in to see that photographer I wore all black head to toe, I had a short spiky Halle Berry inspired haircut, I put the extra touches on my makeup, and came with portfolio in hand. I looked like someone who had flown in from New York, fresh off another set, and could easily come and add substance to the job.

As I entered Ameen Howrani's eclectic studio, I was greeted by the face of every basketball, media personality, and performance artist you could think of gracing his wall of fame. One picture that really stuck out to me was his signature piece – a mahogany mature man adorned in a hat with a flame of smoke coming out of his cigarette. As I waited in the lobby of the studio to meet with him I remember feeling somehow at home.

Meeting Ameen upon first glance you could tell he loved what he did and his studio was a reflection of his journey that he shared through the lens. As I confidently handed my portfolio to him as if I had been doing my job all my life, underneath my clothing I was sweating so profusely that I felt like I had just finished a workout!

Before opening the portfolio he asked several meaningful questions, questions that you know will determine your fate. After looking at each page, he closed my portfolio and said "Don't ever show this to anyone again". I was floored. But what came next would change my life forever. "But you know what, I like you and I'm going to give you a chance". He then picked up the phone and called one of the number one ad agencies in all of Michigan and told them he had a lovely artist that they needed to know and book.

From the time of that interview with Ameen, to meeting with the advertising company, to getting booked on my first job was all of 7 days. Within 30 days I was walking back through Ameen's doors working on an ad campaign *with* him. Within 90 days, my work was in national ad campaigns, magazines, on hair color boxes and on billboards.

I now had work to put in my portfolio that didn't suck, and more than that, the beginning of a lovely working relationship with an awesome group of people – much more than what I could have imagined.

Years later, Ameen told me he could tell I had "it" when I walked through the door. Although my portfolio was not as strong as what that caliber of opportunity required, studying for the role, looking the part, and having the tenacity and audacity to go in and get the role were the driving forces that spoke louder than even the work (and of course I know God was also working on my behalf!).

Working with the advertising company and with Ameen was the kick-off to a string of great jobs with great people, and put me in the position to be able to truly grow as an artist. It all started with the boldness of wanting that role, and being in action to go and get the role.

Thank you Ameen Howrani for giving me my first big break. Thank you Campeau Advertising for providing the wonderful opportunities and platform that allowed me to spread my wings as an artist.

Day 3

What Story Are You Telling? 30 Seconds is All You Have To Tell It!

Storytelling: The interactive art of using words, and actions to reveal the elements and images of a story while encouraging the listener's imagination.

We all love a great story. The power of a great story can take us back to a memorable time in our lives, change our perspective, make us fall in love, dream again, or empower us to make a decision in our lives. A great story makes us believe that what we see is in some way, real, and allows us, if only for that moment, to identify with what the writer wants to share.

Did you know your image is telling a story as well? Only you are the writer, and how effectively you communicate your story determines how well you will be perceived.

Your appearance is your story; it is what people see first and often how they will form opinions regarding you. There is no one I know that is not subjected to making a first impression – from the business professional to the soccer mom, you will constantly be judged through first impressions.

My pastor used an analogy that was so memorable and thought provoking regarding how we live our lives. To summarize it, he asked one simple question – "If your life was a silent picture would people be able to know what you stand for based off of what you do, and the spirit in which you do it?" I often think of this analogy when it comes to your personal image. I believe that your image is always telling a story about who you are; from your hairstyle, the jewelry you select, to the way you smile at people. You are displaying what you feel about yourself and leaving an impression on the minds of all you encounter.

That story is told in the first 30 seconds of meeting someone.

Social psychologists studying the impact of image have determined that someone meeting you for the first time will make up to 10 decisions or judgments about you within the first 30 seconds. These include your economic and educational levels, trustworthiness, social position, level of sophistication, economic heritage, social heritage, and success and moral character. What's amazing is it's not a conscious process, we don't even realize we're doing it. It's a natural process that kicks in during the daily encounters we participate in.

When you meet someone face-to-face, 93% of how you are judged is based on non-verbal data – your appearance and your body language. Only 7% is influenced by the words that you speak. In fact, research about first impressions at Harvard University concluded that we make an in-depth and long-lasting impression in a mere two seconds. Perhaps more surprisingly, the first impression is seldom subject to change.

**Your audience won't get an impression from you,
they get an impression from the image you decide to project.**

While it's true that you don't get a second chance to make a first impression, you do get twenty chances to make up for it. It takes another twenty further experiences with somebody to change a first impression. But all of the subsequent experiences are largely influenced by that first impression, which is why you have to know how to capitalize on the first 5-7 second window of opportunity. That means if you blow the first impression, you have to spend the next 20 moments with the person to prove your worth, that you are the candidate for the job, that even though you seemed mean you really do have a sense of humor, that even though the jacket is too tight, it probably doesn't signify that you don't care. You get the picture; you have to reassure them that their first impression is wrong; that what you are giving off is not true. What a waste of energy that could be better spent closing the deal in other ways!

Why go through all of that when so much is at stake?

For those who represent their own business, having the right look and a great first impression could mean the difference between the resources for your child to attend the school you both desire, whether you win the bid over your competitor, or if you get the ever-changing television gig that will put your company on the map. For others, it's simply a foot they need in the door.

The fact remains, let nothing stand in the way of getting your message to the world, or getting the opportunity to at least be a participant in the game – and that nothing includes your image.

How well you tell the story, how authentic your image is to who you truly are, will let the person who perceives you know what you stand for, and give you a fair opportunity to develop a relationship.

In a world where people can click to multiple pages on a website all with in one minute; when we have so much in our reach in terms of what we are exposed to, there's never been a greater time to make sure that your image is telling your story, an image that speaks of your brilliance and shows you at your best when it counts.

This is usually the point when a few of you might think, "Well that's why I'm really good at what I do, what I look like should not matter." My answer to that thought is that's why it's even more important, because you want to do that which you are brilliant at with the highest mark of excellence as possible, and part of doing your job well is getting to "yes".

So look at telling your story through your image as a means to an end – to make the impression you want to pitch your product, get the promotion you seek, or gain an audience with your target market. Use those 30 seconds wisely, and make every one of them count!

Day 4

Perception is Reality – Yours and Theirs, Especially When it Comes to Your Visual Brand

Perception: The way in which something is regarded, understood, or interpreted

What's perceived is believed

I have always been intrigued with the phrase "perception is reality" because it's so true. What people *perceive* is usually what they believe, and it is based on what they see, hear and think.

Although perception may be reality, I believe you create your reality. How you view things, and yourself, becomes real to you. Once that belief is real to you and what you project, it becomes real to others. But it starts with the first letters in reality, which spell REAL – you have to be real with yourself and what you want first. If not, then you move into a false reality, because what you do comes from an inauthentic place, therefore, you are living someone else's reality. That's why it is so important to define what perceptions you want to leave before you interact with people, and be clear that it is an authentic expression of who you really are.

Our perception of something or someone also extends to the value we place on their worth, also known as perceived value. In business, the perceived value is what the consumer believes the product is worth. The consumers perceived value of goods or service affects the price they're willing to pay; which is in turn based of the way the product is marketed and how much the product "appears" to be worth to them. To extend the discussion of perception further, as it pertains to positioning and our careers, we ourselves could actually be looked at as " product" and through our work, we also produce product(s).

A good example of perceived value can be easily demonstrated through perfume campaigns. In these campaigns a glamorous celebrity is often associated to create this perception of luxury, and because quite honestly we want to duplicate or be like that celebrity – it works for sales. The perfume company may create elaborate and expensive ad campaigns just so they can create a strong image for the perfume or one that speaks of a luxury. The consumers really don't realize the cost of production of the perfume is pretty low. So while the cost of the production for the perfume may only be a few dollars, the perceived value of the perfume could be far greater. Why? Because the reality is we *want* to smell and look like Beyoncé or Halle and in some way by buying this perfume I get a glimpse, a smell, of what their life is like.

So consider yourself a product. What is your perceived value? What value do you place on your image?

One thing that plays a big role with people's perceived value is a brand name. Brand name clothing always sell more than names that are not popular – consider yourself the brand. The better you articulate the look and value of your brand, the more it will assist you in receiving the roles you want.

Remember perception is reality – but you have the ability to change your story, and it's perception.

Perception doesn't stop with those that perceive us; it also plays to how we perceive ourselves. In fact, it starts with us. If we feel like we look like a million bucks, we usually demonstrate it, and if we are self-conscious, it shows as well. So when you look good to others, most often, you look good to yourself. That increased confidence, or a simple compliment from others, could help you to exude more confidence when you interact in your role.

Who wrote the story you are currently living?

I want you to think about the story you're living right now. Who wrote it? Did you consciously decide to create the reality you're living now, or was it mainly shaped by external events that have been internalized? If you don't like the story you are living, then change the perception. Open yourself up to exploring how you'd write the next chapter of your story and what it looks like. If you need to focus your perception on creating a new reality, give yourself permission to start the rewrites – today.

Begin to take responsibility for what you want to present to the world, and the value of you. If you don't begin to shape a true perception of yourself, believe me, others will do so for you.

Day 5

Stars Are Made! Become the Celebrity of Your Business and See if People Don't Start Giving You Red Carpet Treatment!

Celebrity: The state of being celebrated, which brings distinction, eminence, and stardom.

A Celebrity is....

The most admired images and personas of celebrities and brands have simply been crafted and created.

When you see someone that is truly "packaged", much thought and planning has gone into what they want that person or product to reflect, what they are selling, and what feeling you take away from encountering the person on television, in film, or when you see them in person.

Once they have come up with a plan to create the next Beyoncé, Brad Pitt, or Katy Perry, then they go back and gather a team of experts that will see the vision of the image they want to create and have the capacity to invent that image.

Once the image is created, then it is displayed and promoted in everything dealing with that product/person: their look, their promotional materials, and their speech.

They have taken a very detailed approach to assuring that the celebrities' image and persona matches the audience's expectations, and that they look the part of the role they are playing – all the time.

It's then the celebrities job to embody the created image and consistently maintain the persona. The celebrity knows that how well they embrace their image and display confidence affects the next role they get, awards they receive, and if you, their audience, will embrace them.

So how does that apply to you and I? How can we create the same convincing, packaged, and polished look that will accelerate our business, increase our credibility, and allow us to stand out in what we are doing and pursuing?

I believe that you are the celebrity of your business and your life.

You are your brand.

You are the CEO and the Director of your own project – You.com.

Virtually every celebrity in Hollywood has at least one thing in common: they (or their team) are highly skilled at marketing, and branding in particular. Sure, there is luck involved in becoming an A-lister, not to mention talent and genetics. But undoubtedly, image has a great deal to do with celebrity.

Throughout this 40 day journey, we are going to take a look at the marketing strategies and techniques that celebrities use to build their career. You will easily see how you can apply these same strategies to your life to shape your own celebrity status.

7 Ways To Become The Celebrity of Your Business

1 – Figure out what sets you apart.

Celebrities have an "it factor", and they use it to set them apart

Have you ever heard of a "generic" celebrity? Of course not, they all pretty much stand out for special skills they demonstrate. When they fully understand what that it factor is, they ride it till the wheels fall off! As a business owner, it's up to you to identify what makes your business different from everyone else. It could be your years of experience, the customer experience you provide, a unique perspective – but it's YOUR it factor. Work hard to figure out what it is so that you can do more of it.

2 – Dress for the job you want, not the one you have.

Celebrities have a signature look and they look like "stars" .So what exactly makes an actor a star? I can tell you first hand that no celebrity waits until they are famous to start dressing and acting the part. That doesn't fly in Hollywood, and neither does it work in every day life and business. If you expect to become a force in your role, you need to act like one—starting now!

3 – Leverage opportunities for exposure, and learn how to market yourself

Celebrities are skilled at promoting their brand and great at leveraging the media. Celebrities are a product, and they are experts at marketing themselves. No matter your profession, both professionally and personally, we are in essence selling our brand and ourselves. At the end of the day we hope that our brand is strong enough or has made enough of an impression that people buy in to what we are promoting.

4 – Learn ways of evolving and reinventing yourself to change or enhance the opinion of what you do in the eyes of those you want to influence.

Celebrities know how to reinvent themselves for new roles or elevated positioning. Tired of being cast as an extra when you should have the leading role? You can promote yourself through reinvention! How many times have you seen people that are in your industry that have half of the talent you may have, but seem to get more opportunities? Now I know there's such a thing as brown nosing, but what I have found more often that not, that the people who are really good at what they do sometimes get looked over because of three things: their attitude, exposure, or their image. When a celebrity is looking to get better or more challenging roles, they reinvent their image, take acting classes, and begin to expand their circle of influence. What emerges is a reinvented version of them that signifies to the world to take a look at the new me.

5 – Be in touch with your audience, client, customer, and be grateful for their support.

Celebrities never forget that it is their fans that ultimately make them famous. At the end of the day, it's the fans that make celebrities who they are. Without millions of fans lining up to support the celebrities films, music, and products, the celebrity could not thrive, no matter how talented they may be. In business, the same is true of your customers. Always remember that your customers support your business. Let them know you appreciate them.

6 – Embrace collaboration and networking with a purpose.

Celebrities routinely endorse or partner with causes and charities. And while this usually reflects a sincere passion, it's also an excellent opportunity for celebrities to align themselves with causes that they care about as well as generate exposure for themselves. When you know how to give back you begin a process that always returns back to you.

Find groups of people who are on a similar path and look for ways that you can be of benefit to each other. Whether it's to bounce ideas off each other in a think tank, or to refer each others services – good collaboration is invaluable.

7 – Find your authentic voice, be yourself, and own your power.

Celebrities have their own unique "brand" that attracts people to them. How would you like to be so sure in who you are that through your confidence and clarity you attract exactly the opportunities you want to you?

Celebrities are forced to live with their lives as open books. Through having an instant "voice" they express themselves in their own way. Rather than conform, they usually choose to be themselves, and when they do, we all show up to listen and applaud. Through them being discovered and honing their craft, we are often inspired through their work. They decide to fully explore their talents and skills and put it on display for the entire world to benefit from.

Celebrities have something to say, and they say it in their own creative way. They are willing to put themselves on the line for their creative expression.

So can you.

Which six celebrities do you most identify with by their appearance, personality, or acting style? List 4 words that describe them.

Day 6

My "A-Ha" Moment –
"Dude, I AM the Brand!"

A-ha Moment: A moment of clarity, a defining moment where you gain real wisdom; wisdom you can use to change your life. An instant at which the solution to a problem becomes clear

I spent 20 years as a celebrity makeup and hair artist. In that time in the industry I have been fortunate to go to beautiful places, work with talented people who I admire, and experience the fulfillment that comes from seeing my name roll in the credits of movie and television projects.

When I started out as a celebrity makeup artist, I was newly married, had no children living in the house, and life looked quite different. At that time traveling across the country or working on set for long hours seemed exciting, and I embraced working on multiple projects. In the beauty industry, one of the ultimate goals is to work with celebrities, and even more so to be a personal artist to a celebrity – oh the stature it could bring! I always felt the beauty of living that side of artistry was that you could experience "Hollywood" so to speak, and still take off your cape and go home to what was your real world.

But through the years as my family began to grow and the children started getting older, I realized that the same lifestyle of living 12, 13, sometime 14 hour days away from home didn't quite fit what I wanted anymore. With each assignment, I found myself more and more yearning to be at home, to have those special moments in my son's life, and enjoy time with my husband.

I began to feel what many us feel when we become displaced from where we currently are, can sense our desires changing, and are wondering, what next?

It seemed as if the way that I felt really began to intensify and come to a head while on a multi-week tour. It was definitely a highly coveted spot I held on this tour, extremely prestigious, one that I was hand picked to be a part of. What this tour provided was more than just a job – it literally was my personal a-ha moment. It was the moment in time when I realized something that would revolutionize the way I saw myself, and the way in which I saw myself serving the world.

At the end of every night on this tour, there would be a big parade. The music, flashing lights, and colorful costumes would always let me know it was time to call home to my son and to sing his favorite song, which was our bedtime ritual. This night was different, because as I sung to him, what stuck out amongst all of the floats was the child standing next to me. This young boy, about the same age as my son, watched the floats go by in excitement with his Mom holding one hand, while in the other hand he held tight to his cotton candy. At that very moment the prestige and the money of the job did not seem worth missing one more moment with my family. Suddenly the voice of a famous makeup artist came to me who told me when I first started out about what she wished she could change in her career. She said she would have spent more time with her daughter who was now an adult and had no time for her. She also said she wished she realized then that the years go by so fast in a child's life; you have to make yourself present for them. She said she realized now, after the fact, that she could have moved those photo shoots around, or did more jobs at home. Now, she lives in a state of regret for the time she can never regain with her daughter.

That was the night that would begin the quest to put the pieces together as to what my next move would be in my career. I thought surely there was a way to take all that I knew and still live a life that was in integrity with what was important most to me- my family.

Have you ever been in the place where things just didn't seem to fit in to what you really wanted, and at that moment you knew things HAD to change?

Many of us identify with this because we could be in places in our lives where we know something just isn't right.

For me, that night at the parade was a definite turning point. The amazing thing is that if you will be open to hear the answer, God will present to you solutions that you may have never had the ear to hear before. The next day it seemed as if I saw the world differently, and specifically the job I was doing.

With new eyes I now saw that I wasn't promoting simply a brand of cosmetics, the true gold was that I was actually consulting and giving each one of my clients an experience that changed the way they looked at themselves. Suddenly I truly saw the impact that made my experience with these women different and life changing as their confidence was increased, they left feeling empowered, and educated.

I showed them what was possible.

I consulted hundreds of women throughout the course of that tour. As I watched each client walk away from me anxious to implement everything that I consulted them on, I realized that those women would forever be a loyal customer to that brand.

But who was responsible for the experience?

MUAH!

I was the factor in their experience. I realized, at that moment, I had found my NEXT move – helping people truly discover what was possible in their image.

When the revelation came to me, at that moment, I realized I *could* have it all. I could do what I love, but do it on my own terms, completely. From that moment, I started evaluating every piece of valuable knowledge and experience I had ever had in my career and used it to springboard my visual branding company.

I encourage you to not edit the feelings of "what's next" that may be calling you to a new level of greatness where you can have it all. Don't be afraid to reevaluate your roles, what you do, what you like and the things you don't like in your current life. Who says you can't absolutely love what you do, get compensated well for it, and not miss a beat of family life?

I am so absolutely grateful for my "a-ha moment". If I had never had that moment I would never be sitting here writing this book today.

What's you're "a-ha" moment? Do you recognize it? Have you ignored it? It's okay to want it all, if done strategically, you can design the life that you have imagined.

It is possible.

Day 7

Now Starring YOU!
You Are The Brand, And
It's Your Time To Shine!

Brand: A brand is the set of expectations, memories, stories and relationships that, taken together, account for a consumer's decision to choose one product or service over another. – Seth Godin

**You are the star of your life –
and stars were made to stand out and shine!**

I have to imagine that every time a curtain goes up, or the music starts playing, and the performer knows it's time, for lights, cameras, and action, they still get the same butterflies they got the first time they began performing. Despite their fear, perspiration, and angst, they know, at that very moment, they have to rise to the occasion, and let their star shine. Truth is, those who become stars always stood out in some kind of way even before they were discovered. They always had some kind of star quality, and had to make the decision to step forward and pursue that which they were destined to accomplish. The key point that I want to emphasize is that they *decided* to shine, and to shine meant they had to allow themselves to be different and not be afraid of going against the crowd.

I've noticed a common thread running through every successful person ... they are "stars" in their own right and have a very specific way of standing out from the crowd. They become unapologetic about letting their personality shine through, and often times take the road less traveled.

When these "stars" choose to stand out and shine, they are rewarded with their own form of "fans" in new customers and those that subscribe to their brand. Because they choose to pursue passion and are authentic by doing so, they get noticed.

**There is simply is no competition in the lane of
being yourself and letting your own star shine!**

A person who takes the stand to be the star in their lives is comfortable with who they are, and projects the confidence to be unique and let their individuality shine. Standing out from the crowd means that you're not afraid to speak your mind and to avoid following others when to do so results in you feeling as if you are selling out to yourself and your brand.

A person who stands out from the crowd may be someone whose appearance is striking in some way, not because they look like they came off a runway, but because they feel confident in their own skin – and it shows.

While I know that the thought of stepping out and playing big in your image and in your life may seem a bit daunting to some of you, recognize that it does not mean that you have to take a diva persona, become high and mighty, or wear 6 inch stilettos to the PTA meeting. What it means is that you take a stance that you will become the expert in, and represent the brand of you. That decision is what makes you a star and that is what makes you the lead character in the movie of your life.

Decide what standing out from the crowd and shining means for you.

Standing out from the crowd and shining means embracing your individuality and trusting that your own choices are good ones. The person you're projecting out to everyone will stand out more successfully if you're fully confident about yourself. Standing out from the crowd could also mean that you march to your own drum, but respect the humanity of others. Standing out from the crowd means that you don't have to go along with what's popular if it doesn't match what you believe. And while standing out is great, also know that you are the sum total of the 5 people you most communicate with, so if you must have a crowd, make sure that those whom you associate with are one's who you respect and admire as well.

Dress for your role and wear what flatters you. Clothing is always speaking. Make sure yours is saying what you want to communicate. Your clothing can make you shine both in a good light, and bad.

Don't be moved by the crowd. I am always so surprised at how much adult peer pressure exists. I watch as people make decisions for the sake of going along with a crowd of people, only later to feel out of integrity about their decisions. I don't say this from a place of judgment, others have influenced us all, but if you want to stand out from the crowd, you're going to need to stop and ask the hard questions, such as "Does this make sense for me? How will this effect what my goal is? In fashion, trends come and go, but quality and classic garments remain the same. Don't be afraid to say no if what others are doing to advance doesn't agree with you, and remember that saying "no" is a complete sentence, no more explanation is necessary!

Take chances, work hard and smart. Risks and chances are the things in life that can catapult you forward into new territory. Many people won't take up the challenge because they're afraid of failure. But failure is not final, it's just feedback! All of the greats have failed, and with that failure gained momentum to do great things. Have faith in what you feel that you are being led to do, and be willing to take risks to shine.

Do things differently. Find new ways to get people's attention and to stay noticed. Facebook and Twitter demonstrated the power of being the first to do things differently and to stand out from the crowd. Today these two sites have the world eating out of the palms of their hands – from the teenager to the mature senior, and big companies alike.

Be Ballsy. Standing out from the crowd and shining often means that you take action while everyone else stands back, wondering or procrastinating on what to do next. If you learn to have the guts to bring solutions to situations quickly and get things done, you place yourself in a position of being different from 90% of the people "talking" about what they are going to do next.

Your stage awaits, the spotlight is set, now it's your time to shine!

Day 8

What (the heck) is a Visual Brand?

Visual Brand: A holistic, most intelligently packaged, outward expression of your authentic self.

As I started to make the transition from celebrity artist to my coaching and consulting business, I did so by up-leveling my own brand which also included authoring a book – this is where I had another "huge" "a-ha" moment!

When I decided to write my book, I did so on a more than "shoestring" budget! Yet, I was determined that I could use what I knew to promote the book – in fact, I HAD to rely on my own efforts.

I set out to write a killer press kit, create a website that would tell my book's story – in essence, I was determined to look like a best selling author, and look like I had a team of publicists, managers, and a full staff – even though it was little ole me, the support of my family, and endless hours of social media.

In a very ballsy moment, I entered my book into a contest for "Book of the Week" on one of the top nationally syndicated radio shows which in it's own right had millions of listeners! The prize? One week of marketing on all of the radio shows social media outlets, being featured on their website, AND being a guest on the show!

This was media GOLD – especially for a self-published author like myself!

Well – you guessed it – I WON! In fact, after I finished screaming, and I could finally hear the producer's instructions to me, she said some words that would revolutionize my way of thinking. The producer told me they choose me not only because they thought their listeners wanted to hear my subject manner, but because I LOOKED like a brand, I LOOKED like a best selling author, they were very impressed with my press kit, and the way I presented myself on my website!

I looked the part of the author, and therefore – I won over thousands of entries because I stood out from the crowd. Visually branding myself in that new venture was an integral part of gaining press that I could not buy!

From that point on, I felt obligated to not only help people with their images, but also, to empower them to tell their stories in everything that represented them visually. I KNEW, from experience, that she who looks the part, gets the part. Needless to say, I have been able to use this technique to help visually brand everyone from top leaders in the business industry to the most innovative and respected speakers – and I LOVE what I do!

What is a Visual Brand?

The Brandi Mitchell definition of a visual brand is: a holistic, most intelligently packaged, outward expression of your authentic self.

Much more than image consulting alone, my role as a visual brand strategist is to be a visual problem solver and think strategically to get what you are projecting, and who you are, inline with each other to benefit you the most both personally and professionally. At the Visual Branding Institute, we specialize in understanding and conveying your images story so that you can be empowered in your role and be positioned to fully exhibit your star quality in your business and in your life.

Talent alone is not enough to really succeed.
Many people have talent, we all know that.

You may be talented, but if you're not packaged in such a way that it truly connects with others, then you're not going to make your strongest impression and attract the opportunities and roles that you deserve.

Visual Branding is about visually expressing your brand anytime, anyplace, anywhere. It means you directly and subliminally communicate the brand by visually representing it with simplicity, consistency and repetition.

We will talk more about how to truly establish your visual brand later on in the book, but for now, here's a sneak peak into the six steps of creating your visual brand (just a little food for thought to hold you over!).

6 Key Aspects of Creating Your Visual Brand

1. Start with the question of who am I , and what do I want to project?
2. Create a visual style through my 4 step process : Access, Define, Visualize, Create
3. Develop a compelling promotional package –Package yourself like a celebrity
4. Consistently convey your visual brand – In Person, Online, Marketing Materials, Headshot, and through your Supporting Staff
5. Own Your Role & Rock it
6. Learn to live in maintain (your visual brand that is), and don't be afraid to evolve.

Day 9

Great At What You Do,
But Not Getting Paid
What You're Worth?
Maybe It's Time To Find
Out What Your Role
Really Is Or Is Not!

When an actor is developing his character in a production, his goal is to become the character. In order for that process to happen, the actor asks himself three questions to understand the mind of the character he is playing. The actors goal is to put all of their energy and effort into embodying the whole nature of the character to be believable to the audience.

As the star of your business and life, ask yourself these questions to discover what it is that you, the character really wants for your role.

#1 What does my character want? Where do you want to go in life, business, and relationships?

Picture yourself as the character in your own life story. As you begin to answer this question, I want you to answer it from the place of what you actually want, not from the place of what is possible based on where you stand today. Often times based off of our fears, circumstances, and past failures we will "edit" our thoughts of what we actually want. We will slice and dice that very desire to a place that is comfortable for us, or seems attainable. If the thought even survives, it is but a fraction of what we could actually achieve. So just for a moment I want you to think about what your character wants without fear; simply allow yourself to speak what you actually want to do. Agreed?

"Brandi, I don't have a clue of what my next step could be, how can I start to awaken the giant within?" If you aren't sure how to uncover your purpose, here are some tips to help you get started:

What do you do really well that you could become an expert in, leverage as another revenue stream, or specialize?
Usually my clients originally come to me looking for physical change. That change may first be expressed in their desire for an image makeover, but actually the outward desire for change is a part of an inner conversation that's triggering movement. To begin the conversation, I start with defining where they are going in their career and life and put

them in touch with what's on the horizon. I ask them "what is the thing you do that comes very natural to you that would be difficult for others?" Inside of their gift usually resides untapped opportunities that could bring additional revenue.

Pay attention to what captivates you.
Check out the books you buy, magazines you read, and your favorite show. Observe what you find intriguing about someone else's job. What blogs do you just *have* to read every day? What most excites you, or makes you really upset? Now ask yourself why?

Reflect on past roles and experiences to get clues for your future.
They say that the past leaves clues, so take a look at all of the experience you have racked up on jobs, volunteering, etc. to see if any thing from those experiences remains alive for you today. Sometimes even if you have moved on from a particular job, there might be one skill set you learned from that experience that can take on a life of its own or be re-fashioned into something great. For the roles that no longer serve you in this season of your life, resign to grandfather them out so you can open space for new roles and opportunities to present themselves.

Brainstorm on what your role is.

Get a sheet of paper or poster board and divide it into 3 sections:

"What is my role?"

"What are my future roles?"

"What Roles Do I Want To Stop Doing?"

Put pen to paper and write out at least 20 responses for each question. Do not pause or edit, and do not stop before you get to a total of 60 responses. Your role(s) and purpose *will* make itself known.

Ask those you trust what they think.

Poll your friends and family about your roles, talents, and passions. Ask them what they see as your roles and purpose. Pay careful attention to the answers that resonate with you and make you want to nod your head to agree, or yell "Yes!"

#2 What could be getting in the way of what you actually want?

Ask yourself what could stop you from achieving your goals or future roles. This is very important because once you are realistic with what could prevent you from moving forward, you can then create an action plan and system to counteract it from happening or have the plan to address the issue should it arise.

Here are the top culprits for causing delay in stepping into our roles:

1. Not knowing or taking the time out to know what you actually want
2. Lack of focus on what you want
3. Not setting goals, and if you do, not taking action to make them happen
4. Your thought that it won't work
5. Giving up prematurely
6. Not having someone or something you can be accountable to in reaching your goal
7. FEAR

#3 What tactics will I use to get what I want?
What would it take to give myself a promotion?
What does promotion in my life look life?

When we work in one particular area for long periods of time, or for someone other than ourselves, it can be difficult to break out of the mold to see what's possible if we played bigger. I often hear the frustration that comes from people who feel their work goes unappreciated, or they are not getting paid what they are worth. One of my first responses is how about promoting yourself? What would that look like?

Promotion can come in all forms from gaining a new skill, creating a new program, or reinventing what you do and packaging it in such a way that you get a better return. The main point here is don't wait for someone to recognize or give you anything, position yourself to have control over your destiny and begin to weigh what it would take to make it a reality.

Beginning this thought process will allow you to take stock of what you truly want and see what's possible. And guess what, you get to do it in the comfort of your own home, and on your own terms! You get to decide what you will do with the insights you have received today from your own answers, and you get to choose how you will move forward to truly live and flourish in your role.

The point is to choose!

Day 10

Who Are You Auditioning For? Do You Know Their Script?

Knowing and Looking the Part To Attract Your Target Market, and Opportunities

In order for actors to truly deliver on their characters role, they have to study the script of the production they are performing. It's their job to completely know every element of the piece and how their character is to be received to complement the story being told.

We are constantly in character. We present various sides of ourselves depending on who we are around and the circumstances in which we find ourselves.

When you start talking about our roles, the people who we most definitely have to understand are those who our role affects – our customer, clients, and relationships. They all have a "script"; they have an expectation of what they expect from us, and the more we can master and deliver on their expectations while remaining true to ourselves, the more we will advance in our roles.

Your target audience is the people you want to know about you, such as potential employers, community groups, media, or potential clients. It is very important that you market your visual brand to these people in a way that identifies your credibility and conveys your role in a way that is attractive.

When I talk about "getting the role", I'm not talking about faking anything or pretending to be someone you're not. It's actually quite the opposite; the more you project who you are through your image, the more you will resonate with the people you are meant to serve.

LOOK THE PART TO GET THE ROLE is all about dressing as you want to be seen – whether it be serious, professional, upward-bound, artistic, or as a mogul, to ultimately win the roles you want in life. But to win the roles, you have to give a great performance, you have to know your target audiences script!

Researching the Look of Your Role – The Role Assessment ™

To begin to fully understand what your role looks like, take my Role Assessment

#1 Who is your role trying to reach? These are the people that are waiting for you to show up and immediately identify with what they need. Visualize your idea work situation that would make you the happiest every day.

#2 Size up your role. If you want to be a manager, check out what the successful managers in that industry wear.

#3 Check out your role's stars. How do they present themselves? What differentiates them from every one else?

#4 What would the people you are auditioning for expect of your appearance? From luxurious, casual, corporate, out-of-the-box, organic, to straight-laced. You have to look at what your audience will ultimately expect from you and then you begin to live out that role inside of the clothing that you wear.

#5 What does your role make you do? i.e. attend meetings, speaking, presentation, sales, travel, heavy media exposure

#6 Where does or will your role take you? What type of atmosphere, specific events, locations, types of people

#7 What's the persona of the role? i.e. professional, laid back, artsy, corporate, powerful, sporty, earthy

#8 What do you like or dislike about the image of those who are auditioning with you? (The competition, your peers, the people at the top of their game in your industry)

#9 How much of a stretch is the role you are pursuing from where you currently are in your image?

#10 What is the one thing you need to do first to significantly embrace the role in which you occupy or want to pursue?

Know your Role, and Play it Well!

Day 11

What's Your Roles Story?

When visual branding goes right, what happens is that you get to tell your story on your own terms. You have the wonderful opportunity to create the look and feel of your story, tell your story to your audience, and look fabulous doing it! Your visual brand story is a personal one, and when told authentically, can help you relate more effectively and gain access to those you wish to have relationships with.

When you visually tell your story through your image, in essence you are communicating through your physical being, marketing materials, and presence; "Let me tell you about myself without saying a word".

What makes a story stick is it's ability to be memorable. Remember earlier in the book I talked about the impact we have in the first 30 seconds of meeting someone, well depending on how well and how consistent you tell your roles story will determine if you indeed become memorable to those you encounter.

The Ingredients of a Great Visual Brand Image Story

1. A great visual brand story delivers an immediate perception – Not lukewarm, but very much on target whether your role is earthy, a mogul, or artist. The key is to choose a side and stick to it.
2. A great visual brand story displays confidence upon first interaction.
3. A great visual brand story passes the "Scan Test" – When someone looks at you from head to toe, there isn't anything that sticks out so much that it makes their eye focus in on that object – your image flows from head to toe like fluid water.
4. A great visual brand story exhibits and is consistent with the personality of the role – If you come in looking like a diva, don't open your mouth and sound mousy, or lack the ability to make eye contact.

5. A great visual brand story is authentic, authentic, authentic! If you are uncomfortable in any way with your image, it will show, from wearing heels that are too high, to bangs that are irritating to you because you just got them cut. Strive to feel good in your own skin, or learn to adapt to your new roles image.

6. A great visual brand story is consistent and does not contradict what your position is – in other words if you are the boss, you look like the boss!

7. A great visual brand story has marketing materials and websites that are a continuation and extension of the story being told in person.

8. A great visual brand story is consistently sending the same message all of the time – Environments can change, but the essence of your roles look still has a common thread woven throughout clothing, presence, and online.

9. A great visual brand story makes the onlooker want to know more about you, your role, or stay in touch.

10. A great visual brand story radiates credibility and trust.

What story are you telling?

Day 12

What's Your "It" Factor? Uncovering and Stirring Up Your "Secret Sauce"

Secret Sauce: Special skills, products, or abilities you possess that sets you apart.

I am sure you've heard it or either said it about someone else; "She's got it!" Well that "it" is the 'It Factor' also known as your secret sauce. The secret sauce is the attractive quality that someone exudes which makes you want to listen to what they have to say, get to know them, do business with them, or even promote them. Sometimes it becomes very hard for the person who is the receiver of your "it factor" to determine exactly what "it" is, but *you* need to be aware of what it is, and work to do more of it, all the time!

On stage, many of our favorite celebrities know their "it factor" and they make sure they ride it till the wheels fall off. They work it in all they do; it's their mojo.

Having worked amongst artists, as well as those who have that extra charisma to move crowds, I often see how those who have identified their secret sauce know how to use it whether on stage or on the job.

When identified correctly, ones secret sauce allows us to standout in a crowd, have a waiting list of clients, and grab the attention of those who can advance us in our roles.

The it factor has been wildly misinterpreted to focus only on the way someone looks, but indeed it is not only the nature of presenting yourself as attractive as possible – that in fact is just one component. Your secret sauce and "it factor" is discovered when you truly hone in on what you do with extreme ease, what your clients and co-workers always refer to you as "the expert". It's the thing that you are known for, you know, that thing you do that everyone likes. It is that one essential ingredient that sums up your ultimate contribution to the world.

Don't mistake your secret sauce for what you do only; it's also the manner in which you do it. Imagine instead that your secret sauce is the one thing that really makes you special.

Don't worry if you can't easily identify your secret sauce, that can become more apparent in time, what is important is that you begin to find unique things that set you apart from others, and communicate its benefits in all you do.

Your special sauce can be:

- A special skillset
- Experience
- Personal characteristics (research focused, an implementer, easy to initiate conversations)
- Other soft skills (leadership and communication skills).
- And yes, sometimes it is your charisma

4 Steps to Discovering Your Secret Sauce

1. Do a self-inventory, and don't be modest: Examine all the bits that make up who you are: your passions, values, skills, strengths, weaknesses, motivations and goals. Take note of what you really do well, and find the most powerful way to describe it. If you need to picture yourself describing someone else because you are humble, do so, but don't hold anything back.

2. Directly ask your customer or someone that knows you: Ask questions that deliver insightful answers like, "Why have you worked with me for the last 5 years?" or "If you were referring my services, what would you tell them about me? Be sure to write down the answers so that you can do more of what makes you stand out.

3. Look for patterns: Where are the intersections and overlaps that have occurred in your past roles? What kind of patterns do you see?

4. What have you experienced that gives you special insight into a particular group or niche: Think about special points of view you have that could make you invaluable to your role. For example, one of the components of my secret sauce is that I interned in a television studio and learned how to package film and television products. That unique skill set allows me to have insight that most personal branding or image consultants have never experienced – the ability to be able to package what my clients do.

Once you discover what your secret sauce is, make a point to measure the ingredients every 6 months to ensure consistency so you deliver the same quality product every time.

Day 13

Your Life Is a Stage, Get in Character and Stay Focused

All the world's a stage, and all the men and women merely players: they have their exits and their entrances; and one man in his time plays many parts, his acts being seven ages. –William Shakespeare

Your life is your personal stage and now its time to perform. You get to choose your performance and create your story, so whether you're saying a few lines, or whole monologue, the stage is all yours, and it's time you let your audience know that you are there.

No matter what script you've been given, whether life is "going well" or not, your job is to play your role and give your best performance. We co-create the script of our lives. Some choices are ours; others are assigned. Your job is to be confident enough to be seen and heard, but your PURPOSE of your role is to serve the audience.

Even if the road gets hard and you're not sure when you'll win your next role, you keep on playing because you value the experience and it means something to you.

Choose to participate in your life

It's your choice to proactively live out your role, instead of reacting to life. We can live our lives two ways: we can let it coast by before our eyes or we can participate fully. We can't remain outside ourselves and let life happen to us, we need to jump in and get right smack in the middle of things. Of course it's easier to step aside, it's more comfortable to take a passive stance. However it's the road less travelled that allows life's events to unfold. To take control and jump right in we will make mistakes. But they will be our mistakes, and we will learn from them. When we step into our lives and take ownership of what we have done and what we can do, we get to experience both the good and the bad. But really, it's not all bad, because it all leads somewhere, and it all teaches us something. So when you have a choice to continue down the road of least resistance, or you have a choice to change direction and really truly participate in your life, choose participation.

Engage in inspired participation in your life, choose a role that leads you to engage in something that matters to you, playing it fully and enjoying it. It could be a relationship, an entrepreneurial idea, a creative project, contributing to your community, a friendship, changing your career or a million other things. It's only by making a choice to give a great performance that matters which leads to success that actually means something.

The two most important aspects of performance are having stage presence and preparation

Stage presence. In performance, having stage presence could be the difference between looking like a new comer, or an award-winning performer. Great singers know that you can have a number one hit single, but if you can't hold people's attention with your live performance, you've got no longevity in the music business.

Just as there are many people who are talented at what they do in your area of expertise or environment, the person who has that extra something, and presents it in such a way that is impactful, will win every time over skill alone. That extra something is the way you present yourself, how you sell the product of you, and how well you connect with your client. Wonder why Susie got the job over Martha even though Martha may be more qualified? Susie might be a more pleasurable person to be around, Susie might have gone into the interview and sold her abilities like her life depended on it because she really needed the promotion to support her children; you get the picture, skill alone was not the only factor, it was the overall presentation and inner motivation that led to Susie getting the job.

The most important thing for a song to be good isn't necessarily the singing alone; it's the performance. Whether an artist becomes the next singing sensation has every bit to do with how and what they do on stage and in music videos, that's why it's called stage presence.

Your stage presence has every thing to do with how you present yourself. Every part of your visual brand from your hair, to your promotional pictures represents the essence and presence of you. How well you articulate and connect with your audience will determine if you get the lead roles in life or are cast as an extra role.

Preparation. Strong preparation will also help you combat the intimidating experience of performing before a live audience. The more prepared you are to win the role will ease the frustration that comes with day-to-day life.

Preparation consists of:

Having the systems and tool to have peak performance – Having what you need in place to display and maintain your image through your wardrobe plan, makeup, hair, and accessories.

Deciding to commit – To set clear personal goals and relentlessly pursue them.

Rehearse for your performance several times wearing your "wardrobe", including shoes and the accessories. Get in the habit of consistently display your visual brand.

Believe – Belief in yourself and confidence in your capacity allows you to extend your limits, create your own opportunities and push through performance barriers.

Focus – Everybody basically has the same tools, within a certain industry but the individual that truly wins the role is the one with the most desire and best focus.

Learning to control distractions – Controlling distractions is your ability to maintain or regain a positive focus when faced with potential roadblocks, negative input, or setbacks. These distractions may be external, arising from your environment, or internal, arising from your own thinking or expectations. Maintaining and regaining a constructive focus is a critical part of performing to your capacity on a consistent basis, whether distractions occur before you hit your stage, during the performance, or after life's events. This is made possible by planning to refocus and refine your ability to use reminders to rapidly refocus on what is within your immediate control in the present moment.

Day 14

You Were Created Lovely:
A Star Is Born

Lovely: Having a beauty that appeals
to the heart or mind as well as to the
eye, as a person or a face.

Many times when we think about image transformation or changing our image we think that there has to be something wrong with us. Please let me reassure you that is not what this book is about. I want you to know right now that you were perfectly created by God.

With the 20 pounds, without the 20 pounds.
With long hair with short hair.
No matter your ethnicity, or the color of your skin

You are lovely.

We were crafted in the image of God – and God is beautiful. How can we be anything less than fabulous?

Now what is real is that we can forget just how lovely we are, because perhaps life has told us otherwise, and we choose to believe the opinions of others. Sometimes the voices of others and society can feel as if it drowns out every fiber of confidence we have. But at the end of the day, if someone else tells you a different story – know that the true story is you are lovely.

I teach through my visual branding the importance of being image conscious. Image conscious is being aware of the image you deliver and how you can present the best version of yourself that best conveys who you are. Image is used in that respect to communicate who you are and what you do – it is in fact a tool in your arsenal used for marketing the product of you.

There's a big difference between being image-conscious and being self-conscious

When people are preoccupied with image or become self-conscious, it is actually quite the opposite of being image conscious. When you are self-conscious you are so concerned with everything that everyone else thinks about you that you allow what they think to influence how you see yourself. Being self-conscious can affect everything in your life, from your relationships, to your career, and it will keep you from truly living your best life. When we are self-conscious we focus our attention on the negative rather than recalibrating the negative feelings we may have about ourselves into something positive. It allows us to be controlled by what others think, when our ability to enhance our beauty comes from within.

When you are image conscious, you make a decision to represent yourself in your best light because its connected to what you want, feel, and because it is a form of self expression.

We all have something that's unique about us, things about our appearance that makes us fabulous, things that we can polish up and enhance. We were all made unique for a reason, not to be carbon copies of one another, but to feel comfortable being ourselves. Inside of what makes us unique we find perfection.

Having Confidence is lovely
Having Humility is lovely
Having Fierceness is lovely
Having Integrity is lovely
Having Boldness is lovely
Authenticity is lovely
Having Courage is lovely
Intelligence is lovely
Being coachable is lovely

You are lovely.

Day 15

What 8 Miles Taught Me: The Eight Mile Story That Almost Never Happened

Often times when we are looking to move forward in our lives, the biggest enemy is the *inner me*.

It's those inner conversations you have with yourself that talk you out of what could truly be great. The conversation often is based off fear, past failures, or preconceived notions we may have of what of we *think* will be the outcome.

One of my biggest lessons learned in this area came on the set of a film called *8 Mile,* starring Eminem, Brittney Murphy, Mekhi Phifer, and Anthony Mackie.

A pivotal career move for me that almost didn't happen.

I was a new mother, whose day was filled with diapers, TV, and being in amazement of this beautiful new experience of motherhood. That same year, the twin towers came down, so it was a year that made you truly appreciate every moment and become brutally aware of how you live your life.

One day I got a call about a new film that would feature superstar rapper Eminem in a story loosely based off of his life being shot in Detroit. My first *inner me* conversation was "Not interested, I've worked on rap sets before, and I don't want to be on one for several weeks!" Because of my new role as Mom, I was super sensitive to protecting my world (and still hormonal), so I wasn't even thinking about the fact that this was a major film; that it was simply a story being told. Based on where I was at the time with having a new baby and spending loads of time in the house, the inner conversation that I told myself was that it would be a crazy atmosphere.

I was so absolutely wrong.

A few weeks went by, and I received another call, this time, I was literally handed the job. The conversation went something like this "They are having such a difficult time finding someone that can hold down this position in the hair department, if you want it, the job is yours, and you can start tomorrow, but Brandi please come".

At this point it was becoming pretty obvious this was something I was supposed to do. These are very coveted positions in film; positions that people are fighting to receive, and it was given to me not once, but twice. So I went and talked to the crew and told them everything I could think of ahead of time like, "I have to go pump milk every couple of hours", "I am a new Mom so I'll have to check on my son often" -everything I could think of to make sure I was walking into the right situation. Their response was "of course, do what ever you need, we understand". Not at all the response I imagined during one of my *inner me* sessions with myself.

On my first official day on set, I was greeted by the crew with open arms, taken to get breakfast from craft services, and then my day began. I saw nothing but professionalism, and those honing their craft. All of the inner conversations and assumptions I had were wrong.

While hired as a hairstylist, when the makeup department realized I was also skilled in makeup, they wanted me to do double duty and work with them as well. I remember so clearly one of the artists saying, "Where have you been all this time, do you know how many people we had to go through, and it seemed like you just appeared out of thin air! Where were you?"

I realized at that time that I almost let a really good opportunity go, one that was orchestrated for me from the beginning of the film because of my inner conversations based on fear.

Working on that film was one of the turning points in my career. I saw the film make history to become one of most iconic rap films to ever exist. I worked on the music video for the theme song of *8 Mile* which won an Oscar and whose song became an anthem to many representing perseverance. On that set I got to witness a young man's star rise, who is now a successful actor and Oscar contender, Anthony Mackie, and I met people who I still am in touch with today. I also grew to have a love for film and directing while shooting that same movie.

To imagine that this is the same opportunity I almost talked myself out of because of the negative thoughts that I had in my mind:

- My fear of being able to balance motherhood and career
- My preconceived notion and judgment of the set (which it definitely was nothing but professionalism and a creative atmosphere)
- My questioning of my ability to be able to perform

I had all those *inner me* conversations going on in my head, none of which panned out to be real.

So I ask you, what could possibly be some of the negative *inner me* discussions that could be holding you back from something great? What negative chatter could be blocking you from evolving in your image? What is a conversation that you're having that may be so incredibly loud at this very moment it's holding you back from a breakthrough to the next level of your life? I'm challenging you to go back and revisit the conversations and judge if they are legitimate. Go back and examine what is being motivated by fear, versus what is real to see if you could possibly be missing out on your own "eight mile experience".

I'm so glad that I decided to shut down the noise that was in my head, and pursue the "what is possible" instead.

Lose Yourself.

Day 16

Listening to the "Inner Me": Dealing With The Ten Image Sabotage Personalities™

Conflict: A fight, battle, or struggle, especially a prolonged struggle; strife.

Every good story has conflict; the protagonist has a goal that must be achieved. The conflict is any type of problem that keeps this goal from being conquered.

In our personal stories, the conflict is about what's going on inside us and in our lives. Opposition may challenge us in achieving what we want. The conflict can be internal or manifest itself outward in a physical obstacle like dealing with a weight issue or skin challenge, and/or internal challenges such as low self-esteem, anger, or being stuck in our ways.

One of my jobs as a visual brand strategist is to be a safe place for people to come and transform their image to become the next and best version of themselves. In doing so, I usually come up against patterns and mindsets from people that prohibits them taking themselves any further with their image, so they come to me to help them in seeing what is possible. Along with service to my clients in workshops and consulting sessions, I also talk to people through my weekly e-zine and videos, and find that they too have similar questions regarding breaking through to the next level of their image.

More often than not, a lot of the situations and dilemmas they experience have to deal with this inner conversation driven by one of the Ten Image Sabotage Personalities™ that prohibits them from truly seeing what is possible. To progress to what's waiting for them in their roles, they have to conquer what sabotages their promotion. Awareness that you are indeed sabotaging yourself comes first, and the next step is identifying the problem or the blockage in order for you to bring a solution to the issue.

Taking an honest look at these 10 Image Sabotage Personalities™ in the pursuit of creating your visual brand will help you navigate and work to eliminate issues before they arise. You may find that you are a combination of more than one of the personalities and that's fine, just know that this is not to be judgmental or hurtful, but like they say in church, when you see yourself, just say "amen" or "ouch!" The more honest you can be with yourself in seeing where you are, the further you can go in tweaking and adjusting the mindset that comes along with these things that block us from reaching our goals.

The concept of self-sabotage is essentially the act of hindering your own progress or intended goal.

When you self-sabotage your image, you unconsciously create the very same situations that you are trying to avoid. We may say that change is what we want; yet for reasons we don't understand, we make choices and display habits that negate our efforts.

But what's great is that the sabotage can cease the day you become aware of how you sabotage yourself and make a decision to do things differently. You don't have to stay stuck or frustrated with falling for the ole' banana in the tale-pipe over and over again. For me personally my two Image Sabotage Personalites were The Procrastinator and The Critic, and before I became aware of how much they were affecting me, I was super hard on myself every time I fell short. Once I understood how I sabotaged myself, I consciously set up an answer to address the negative thoughts that came to hinder me from moving forward.

The 10 Image Sabotage Personalities™

The Procrastinator – The Procrastinator says "I'll do it when I lose 20lbs", "I'll start exercising when the weather breaks", "I'll do it for my birthday". They put off what they can do now until they *have* to do it. They sometimes experience a physical rush by having a deadline.

The Emulator – The Emulator is just looking for the next trend, and they don't know exactly who they are so they emulate others or go to the next hot thing, without truly defining what works for them.

The Chameleon – The Chameleon is always feeling like they need to change. They often change their hair, their look, their logos, so it's very hard for them to build a brand and establish a look because they look different in all of their pictures and you never know who may show up.

The Critic – The Critic can be very hard on themselves and *their* worst critic, they are usually hard on others as well. So when the critic fails on a diet, or a picture of them doesn't look well, they will feel the need to punish themselves.

The Out of Touch – The Out of Touch personality is in a bit of a time warp and out of date, so what worked for them in a particular season of life they keep doing even though it may not work for who they are today.

The Over Confident – The Over Confident says, " I'm already fabulous, how could you possibly make me any better?" However, they are not. They are sometimes controlling and resistant to change with a touch of The Out of Touch personality.

The Repeater – The Repeater will do things over and over again, what they're used to; and is stuck in their ways.

The Intellect – The Intellect says "I'm smart and good at what I do, what I look like doesn't matter". Sometimes they even try to dress smart or extremely corporate and down play their appearance so you can know them for their intellect *not* their looks.

The Downer – The Downer thinks that nothing they do will make them look better. The Downer may suffer from extreme low self-esteem, sometimes feeling like they don't deserve to be happy.

The Clueless – The Clueless never had a sense of style the majority of their life, and just needs help and guidance.

Identify the negative chatter and create a different conversation to eliminate the image sabotage by dealing with the issues:

"It doesn't matter what I look like, I'm good at what I do"
- Ah, yes it does! A decision is made on you in the first 30 seconds based off of you image.
- Why not let your visual brand match your brilliance?

"I'll do it when I lose 10lbs"
- The opportunities aren't going to wait until you lose the weight, so you have to create the best version of yourself NOW.

"I don't have money to improve myself"
- You can look fab on any budget, and even shop in your closet once you know what works for you.
- You have to invest in you, and your image gives GREAT returns.
- You can actually get more business and exposure with up-leveling your look.

"I don't want to look "made up"
- There are ways to look polished and enhance your natural beauty without overdoing it.

" I don't want to dress up everyday"
- You have to develop a way of having consistency in your image; that you are polished whether you're running errands or going to a networking meeting.
- You are simply maintaining the basics in grooming your appearance.
- Learn to create a wardrobe that pushes you towards your next level and have a closet full of options that flatter you no matter the occasion.

"I don't have the time"
- You HAVE TO make the time and invest in your image for the greatness that lies ahead, don't let any opportunities get missed by making the wrong first impression.
- By developing a system for being polished, creating a look for yourself, and having elements that help to further that look, you'll find that you actually SAVE TIME.

"It doesn't matter what anyone does to me, I don't think I can be helped"
- Everyone can improve his or her image. Everyone has a way to be polished in his or her own right.
- We have been beautifully and uniquely crafted by God to fulfill our purpose and to let him shine through us. That is true beauty.

Being polished is not about becoming beautiful. It's about polishing off what you have been given, and doing the best with what you have in your current state, right now!

When you stop being able to learn you stop being able to grow. One of the biggest things in moving forward and going to the next level in anything is being able to have the capacity to be coachable, recognizing that you don't know everything, and being open to ways to improve what it is that you do.

So what are some of the ways you may be sabotaging yourself?

You neglect to set up a support system
(The Procrastinator, The Out of Touch, The Repeater)
It is very difficult to reach our goals or to change a habit by ourselves. Whether it is writing a business plan, starting a new workout regimen, or getting rid of the bad habit, we all need support and accountability to someone; a coach, family member, friend, or a mentor. When you can

anticipate where you might need support, you will be more prepared for any situations that happen to come to sabotage your efforts. The most successful people in business, health, and in the spiritual arena know that asking for help is not a sign of weakness, it's necessary to go to your next level.

Fail to celebrate your small successes
(The Downer, The Chameleon, The Critic)

People love to be celebrated, they love to know that what they are doing matters and be recognized. People need to be validated and it helps improve their confidence. But did you know that just as much as people like to be celebrated, we need to hear it for ourselves every once in a while? Celebrate the milestones that you achieve on your way to your goals because they are the roads that take you to your ultimate goal. If you don't take time to celebrate the small things, it is going to be very easy for you lose your motivation to continue to the end.

You rely on your willpower and super-powers
(The Overconfident, The Intellect, The Emulator)

Willpower is an excellent thing to have but is often motivated by a push of energy that later fizzles out. Its strength is that it is driven by extreme determination which in and of itself can sometimes be draining. Because of the rush of emotion, it can be hard to remain consistent, especially for a long period of time or long-term goals. The best way to incorporate willpower and stay motivated to keep yourself from sabotage is to get clear on the reason why you're doing what you doing. When things become challenging and difficult, you can always point back to the reason you're doing what you are doing and that will be what gives you the energy to sustain and stay committed.

You focus on failures
(The Downer, The Critic)

People who have been extremely successful in life all have one thing in common; they have failed several times before they finally made it. They take failure simply as feedback, and use it to fuel them forward. Failing comes only when you completely give up and refuse to try any longer. Don't let your fear of failing sabotage you from moving forward. Should you fail, reflect back on the experience and learn the lessons.

Having no plan
(The Clueless, The Repeater)

The old saying says, "If you fail to plan, you plan to fail." This is extremely true especially for really busy people. The reality is that if you don't write something down and literally plan out time to implement your goal, it really may not happen. Even with the best intentions, in all the desires to want to meet with that client, go out with one of your old friends, or exercise; if you don't actually make time and plan for it to happen, the likelihood is slim to none that it will get done. One of the biggest learning curves for me in my business was understanding that I had to be organized and that I had to make the time to plan to achieve my goals. When you don't have a plan, no matter how good you are at what you do, you are literally sabotaging any success that's waiting for you whether it is personal, physical, or professional. When you fail to plan it also becomes easy for you to get overwhelmed which can make you stop right in your tracks and do nothing.

One of the easiest ways to determine if you're sabotaging yourself is to purposefully observe your self. That's right I said it, take the opportunity to look at yourself without judgment and watch yourself as if you were critiquing someone else. Observe and take note of when you don't feel like doing something or an excuse comes up, and then watch to see what the behavior is that you do afterwards. Was it fear, jealousy, the need to be in control, did you feel the need to lie because the truth did not seem good enough, were you seeking attention? Look to see what was driving the sabotage.

Re-Cap for dealing with the Ten Image Sabotage Personalities ™

1. Identify the ways that you sabotage yourself
2. Understand why you sabotage yourself
3. Make the choice to change and be willing to release what's holding you back and start fresh
4. Experience true transformation and work to reprogram yourself where necessary
5. Celebrate yourself every time you do something to change the thing that sabotaged you
6. Be present to the moment and don't constantly revisit the past
7. Do more of what works well for you
8. Remain coachable
9. Release disappointments from the past or judgments of past experiences.
10. *Believe* in yourself and be authentic along this process. If you lie to yourself, how can you tell the truth to others?"

Day 17

First Take Off the Girdle, and Get Real! Look At Your Image Today

Research done at UCLA on communication found that in a very specific situation where people were communicating about emotions and attitudes, 7% of what came across depended on the content of what was said, 38% of how it was said (the speaker's voice, tone, and accents); and 55% depended on how the person looked when communicating.

LOOK THE PART TO GET THE ROLE is about making you aware of what impression your 55% is making so that you communicate the impression you desire and you can have the most complete visual brand possible.

Get Clear About Your 5 P's

It helps to think about what I call the 5 P's when accessing your visual brand that are:

1. Your PERSONAL image
2. Your online PRESENCE
3. Your marketing collaterals that PROMOTE you
4. How your image POSITIONS you
5. Your total PACKAGING

To do so I have created this Visual Brand Assessment ™.The goal of this self-assessment is to support you in raising your awareness around your image and visual brand that could be creating a source of inconsistency, stress or misrepresenting you and your role(s) in your life. Read each phrase and choose YES or NO for each. If you are not 100% certain on a YES, then mark NO for now.

Grooming

Makeup

I own a set of professional make up brushes that serve multiple functions	YES __ NO __
I know how to apply my makeup no matter the occasion	YES __ NO __
I have my eyebrows shaped great, and maintain them on schedule	YES __ NO __
My makeup lasts throughout the day	YES __ NO __
I feel comfortable with the shade of foundation I wear	YES __ NO __
I feel comfortable applying my own makeup on a day-to-day basis	YES __ NO __

Hair

I regularly receive haircuts or trims	YES __ NO __
I have a color that enhances my haircut	YES __ NO __
My hair is in a healthy condition, and I regularly condition it with good quality hair products	YES __ NO __
I always receive compliments on my hair	YES __ NO __
Because my hair is cut so well, it is easy for me to duplicate and style at home	YES __ NO __

Skincare

I have a skin care regimen that I do everyday including cleansing, moisturizing, and age pre-ventative techniques	YES __ NO __

Should I wear makeup, I remove it every night   YES __   NO __

I use an eye cream   YES __   NO __

I exfoliate my skin at least once a week   YES __   NO __

I always wear sunscreen when needed   YES __   NO __

Clothing

I am fully aware of my body shape, and I dress   YES __   NO __
in a way that flatters it most

I understand how to camouflage any flaws   YES __   NO __
without hiding my entire body, wearing draping
materials, or dressing in dark colors

I don't waste time getting dressed because I have   YES __   NO __
a multi-functional wardrobe where the pieces are
interchangeable and serve me in multiple ways

When I dress, everything flows seamlessly, and   YES __   NO __
I have a total look consisting of makeup, hair,
wardrobe, accessories, shoes, and great self
-confidence

Accessories

I have accessories for multiple occasions   YES __   NO __

I have adequate accessories inside my wardrobe   YES __   NO __
to create different variations of my wardrobe (be
it dressing the clothing up, making it casual, or
fashion forward)

I have shoes that are fashionable   YES __   NO __

Multi Functional Wardrobe

My wardrobe is an honest expression of my true self (ex: colors, clothing, accessories, shoes, etc.).   YES __   NO __

My current wardrobe represents my visions of the role I am and who I want to become, not who I was   YES __   NO __

I wear 80% of the wardrobe in my closet   YES __   NO __

I always feel like I have a flattering and appropriate outfit to wear no matter what the occasion.   YES __   NO __

I often get compliments when I dress   YES __   NO __

Body

Diet

I eat vegetables at least 3 times a day   YES __   NO __

I have a bowel movement within 3 hours of eating   YES __   NO __

I drink half of your body weight in water daily?   YES __   NO __

The food I eat fuels my day, gives me more energy, and does not drain me   YES __   NO __

I detox frequently and safely (ex: herbal teas, cleanses, colonics, deep breathing, etc.).   YES __   NO __

I get the right amount of sleep needed to wake up feeling refreshed and energized (7-8 hours suggested).   YES __   NO __

Exercise

I exercise 3-5 times a week   YES __   NO __

I incorporate strength training in my workouts at least 3 times a week   YES __   NO __

I workout outside when weather permits   YES __   NO __

I can jog and talk without being winded   YES __   NO __

Weight Management

I am at my optimal/healthy weight and I have an abundance of energy to live a full life.   YES __   NO __

I have been on a diet at least once in the last 90 days   YES __   NO __

I have engaged in yo-yo dieting   YES __   NO __

Do feel comfortable at your current weight?   YES __   NO __

Marketing & Branding

Promo Pictures/ Headshots

I have had professional pictures taken in the last 11 months.   YES __   NO __

I have a headshot that is so flattering that it could be attached to any bio, information product, brochure, or editorial feature.   YES __   NO __

I look the same in person as I do on my promotional pictures when I go to an event, am networking or attend a business function?   YES __   NO __

I clearly know what my "it factor" and secret sauce is, what I do, and can communicate it effectively within 30 seconds.   YES __   NO __

My promotional efforts represent who I am today   YES __   NO __

Marketing Materials

I have high quality business card that sells me and speaks to what I do   YES __ NO __

I have a brochure that plainly states every service I offer   YES __ NO __

I have a logo that represents my companies business and attributes   YES __ NO __

My marketing materials represent who you I am today   YES __ NO __

Online Presence

My website has an opt-in box to generate a list of subscribers I can communicate with regularly   YES __ NO __

I regularly communicate to my clients and audience through an email newsletter or blog format   YES __ NO __

I post and have active conversations on social media at least 6 times a week   YES __ NO __

I am actively a part of at least 3 social media platforms (i.e. Facebook, Linked-in. You Tube, Twitter)   YES __ NO __

I utilize video as a marketing tool monthly   YES __ NO __

Day 18

One Of These Kids
Is Not Like The Other

Where are you out of sync
with your current role or the
role that you want?

Reality Check – How Do You Compare? How's it all adding up?

Our visual brand has to have balance, not rely so heavily on one thing, but be a collaboration of ingredients that makes it seamless and work. On Day 17 you identified where you are currently in your image with my Visual Brand Assessment™, today you will put all of your findings in perspective. Take the time to see where are you out of integrity (where you may be the most inconsistent) with your role and what you want based off of the assessment.

Most people have one or more elements that could use some improvement, so throughout the book, and through our programs you can discover ways to improve and begin to upgrade your visual brand. Once your lowest elements are improved, there is a good chance the other elements will fall into place as a by-product because each of the elements impacts each other.

Please rank which quadrant is the most important to YOU to upgrade now (i.e. Grooming, Clothing, Body, Marketing & Branding). Then rate each element on a scale of 1 – 12 to create the order you would like to improve first. (i.e.: #1 would be first to focus on, #12 would be last)

The Visual Brand Assessment ™

12 Elements & 4 Quadrants

Quadrant 1- Grooming	**Your List of Upgrades in Priority**
1. Makeup	1.
2. Hair	2.
3. Skincare	3.
	4.
Quadrant 2- Clothing	5.
4. Dressing for your shape	6.
5. Multi-Functional Wardrobe	7.
6. Accessories	8.
	9.
Quadrant 3 – Body	10.
7. Diet & Detox	11.
8. Exercise	12.
9. Weight Management	

Quadrant 4 – Marketing & Branding
10. Promo Pictures/Headshot
11. Marketing Materials
12. Online & Website Presence

Day 19

Change One Thing Or Do A Complete Overhaul? Where to Start First

Change is in the air

If you're anything like me, when you can sense change is on the horizon, everything starts looking different. I quickly start evaluating how I can make all of the parts in my life accompany the shift that is occurring whether it be in business, a project, or family life. I have found however that all of us take different approaches to change once we are aware of things we need to do.

There are three different ways people tackle change, especially as it relates to up-leveling their visual brand. See where you fit, see what resonates, and determine when and how you will take action.

Do it all er
This is the person who decides to go all in, and jump head first into change. Because they feel like they might procrastinate if they think about it to long, they often try to create change as soon as possible so they won't talk themselves out of what they know needs to occur.

Tackle one side or the other
This person has identified where they need the most help, and will either tackle the physical element of their visual brand like their makeup, hair, and wardrobe, and decide to add to it the marketing and packaging side on their second round. Sometimes they feel so unbalanced on one side or the other that they have to come up to speed with the stronger side to have any kind on normalcy.

One thing at a time
This person might stick their pinky toe in the water but not the whole foot and definitely not their entire body! They might decide to try out one of the 12 elements, and gradually add on the other 11 elements separately.

The Observer

The Observer won't do anything but take all the information in, and will do it later when they have had enough, are at their breaking point, or have a new opportunity that forces them to hurry up and do something quick to prepare. Usually at this point it is more of a necessity as opposed to something they've willfully chosen.

Assess your biggest challenge

After you have taken a look at the results of your Visual Brand Assessment™, I want you to stand in front of the mirror and take a look at yourself. Ask yourself what you feel needs improvement or updating. Is it your clothing? Your headshot? Have you worn the same lipstick shade for the last three years? Do you look older than you are? Work this out, and you will know where to begin your visual brand makeover.

What is pressing in your life, and how bad do you want change?

Are you up for a new project, promotion, an event with your ideal clients, a reunion? What's motivating you? What do your plans for your business look like for the next 90 days, 6 months, 1 year? This will determine your intensity level of your transformation and which approach you take to enhancing your visual brand.

Day 20

Do You Need An Acting Coach? Bringing In Reinforcement and Realizing When You May Need Help

Ask any actor that has experienced a great acting coach, and they'll tell you the value that comes with having someone groom, stretch, and open them up to places in their craft they could never achieve on their own in their careers. From the beginning actor to the seasoned actor trying to break into another arena or genre; to an actor that is on a mission to win an Oscar, all of it requires that they have someone to help guide them to the next level.

Many of the things in this book are made for you to immediately implement into practice in your image. Your next steps that you implement yourself after reading the book will depend on your level of familiarity with fashion and beauty, along with the level of understanding some of the techniques found on these pages. I also recognize that for some this book may be the spark to start the quest in up-leveling your visual brand, and make you seek out personal help to begin realizing your best version of yourself.

The key to growth will be in your ability to be honest with yourself and then make a decision to move forward whether it be with a total transformation or strategic movement in one or two areas that will improve your image.

Reasons some people seek out a coach, or professional for their image and visual brand:

- Problem with visual representation
- Career change
- Going from corporate environment to representing their own brand
- Launch of a new business, project, or platform
- Trouble finding work or getting paid what you are worth
- Desire for a new relationship
- Feeling as if you may not be dressing appropriate for age, profession, or feel it's time to update your image.

- Being put in a position where you will have more visibility in your industry or amongst peers.
- Want to up-level your brand

The benefits of having help to up-level
your image and visual brand

#1 Motivation: You know you need to do certain things to up-level your image, but you may not know where to start or you may procrastinate to the point of frustration. Having someone help you to up-level your image and motivating you to embrace the best version of you will serve as the extra help you need to try that new color of lipstick, wear a different hairstyle, or see yourself as the CEO in your marketing materials. Without the help, we can revert back to what is comfortable.

#2 Accountability: This, hand-in-hand with motivation, are probably the two largest contributors to your success and progression. When you truly begin creating your visual brand and stepping out to say this is who I am, you now put yourself in a place of being accountable to maintain the image you are looking to project to yourself, your audience, and those you have entrusted to help you up-level your image.

#3 Having outside perspective: When we analyze our own image, we sometimes only see what we want to see, however when someone else with a trained eye looks at you and your image, you have a greater chance of getting a better assessment of where you are plus you get solutions. Another factor is that based on our vantage point, we can either be too hard on ourselves or to lenient in judging where we stand in our image, which is why truly having perspective from a professional that is in tune with you and your role is invaluable.

Many of the most successful people get coaches for various stages in their lives. They recognize when they have taken themselves as far as they can, and getting help will shorten the distance to what they want to achieve. What help looks like in terms of your visual brand is a team consisting of makeup artists, hairstylists, personal shoppers, photographers, graphic artists, and web designers, even business coaches. All of these resources are valuable at different times of your visual branding journey to create the brand of you! Learn more about our visual branding solutions at www.brandimitchell.com

Day 21

Seeing IS believing:
Creating a Visual
Storyboard

In film, storyboards are graphic organizers in the form of images for the purpose of pre-visualizing scenes in a film or performance. The storyboard provides a visual layout of events as they are to be seen through the camera lens, and allows a movie director to communicate his vision of the scenes within the movie to other personnel involved in its production. The crew members can visualize the movie's desired look, and better prepare to make it a reality.

In my visual branding process, I created a process I call visual storyboarding to allow both me and my team to have a clear vision of the individuals visual brand and the components to their visual brand story. It's a pretty awesome concept because you can see all the elements of the individuals' role coming to life through pictures, words, and colors, and it really calls into action everything I visualize for the client and tells their story clearly.

When I realized how helpful visual storyboarding was for me in creating the clients vision, I started teaching people to create these visual storyboards for themselves as a part of another class I teach on packaging and pitching your role. The visual storyboard keeps you organized, guides you to stay focused on your goals, and helps you to keep a clear vision of what *you say* you want to look like.

A visual storyboard contains collections of images, illustrations, words, and an actionable plan that visually represent the image you want to convey in your life.

The more concise you can be with expressing where you want to go in your visual brand and telling the story through pictures accompanied by a plan, the closer you are to actualizing your look.

Variations of Visual Story board

Binder: For a binder, you want hole puncher, insertable folder pockets, as well as paper, glue, tape, and other artsy items to include to tell your story.

Book: You can make your visual storyboard portable by using a composition notebook that you can tuck into your bag, or purse.

Digital: You can create a digital visual storyboard on your computer and to keep track of your online inspirations. Use a scanner to import images from magazines or photographs, and keep the file together using a program like iPhoto, or imaging software like Photoshop.

Poster board, corkboard: Probably the most common way to create a visual story board where images and words are attached to the board and the board is hung up for display.

The Tools

- Thick card, poster board of any size, corkboard.
- Magazines of all kinds (you never know where your visions will be found)
- Glue Stick or Double sided tape
- Music – something restful to help your mind be quiet and open

This process of building your visual storyboard will happen over the next 4 days in 4 steps:

Step 1: Creating the foundation of your visual story board
Step 2: Determining the words that describe your visual brand
Step 3: Identifying your role(s) model
Step 4: Creating your action plan

With each day completed you will have another element to add to your visual storyboard. The first day you will create the foundation for the board with the collection of your pictures. The second step will help you to get the words that will serve as visual cues describing the visual brand you are creating. The third step will show you why you naturally gravitated towards particular pictures on step 1 and also help you to put together outfits for your role. The fourth step will walk you through creating an implementable plan to make your image goals a reality.

By the completion of the fourth step you should take some quiet time and construct your visual storyboard fully empowered and enlightened to what your role looks like and the story that will accompany it through clothing, accessories, makeup, and hair choices.

Step 1 : Creating the foundation of your
visual story board – The Gathering Process

A good starting point is flipping through magazines and searching the Internet for inspiration. Begin cutting and printing out all images that attract your attention at first glance; the ones that instantly mean something to you. It's not only fashion, it's nature, shapes, ads, colors, commercials, videos; things that will trigger elements to add to the visual story you want to tell.

You will be looking for visual representation of your image in the following areas:

- makeup looks
- hairstyles
- wardrobe
- accessories
- shoes
- your ideal shape
- fitness goals

- promotional ads you like
- marketing pieces on the internet
- pictures that represent your role
- logos that catch your eyes
- colors and textures that appeal to you

When you are going back through the images, you may find that certain items don't fit in the story you are creating, those will be the items that don't go on the board and are eliminated. If you choose to do this exercise in a group setting at one time, feel free to attach all the pictures, but attach them with temporary items like removable tape or push pins just in case you realize later that they actually may not be an accurate fit.

Tomorrow Ill show you how to add on to your this visual storyboard.

Day 22

What Four Words Will
You Use? The Power of 4

Words are a powerful tool in bringing to life what we imagine into reality. Until we are forced to quiet our minds and without editing our thoughts, think of what we truly want to express, we can go on for months, years, heck, our entire lives without truly defining the mark we want to leave and how we want to be viewed. This exercise is a powerful tool to help you see what you truly want to communicate in your visual brand. Allow yourself the luxury of just saying what's in your heart without having to figure out how it's going to happen – we will get to that later. For now, take the time to answer these questions, you may be surprised at some of the answers!

Today we will be adding on to creating your visual storyboard by incorporating Step 2 in the 4-step process:

Step 2: Determining the words that describe your visual brand – Exploring the power of 4

The four words you would like people to take away as a first impression of who you are after meeting you are:

1.

2.

3.

4.

The four words to describe the way you want to look are:

1.

2.

3.

4.

The four words to describe the clothing you wear are:

1.

2.

3.

4.

The four words to describe the benefit of what you do in your role are:

1.

2.

3.

4.

The four words to describe the life you live are:

1.

2.

3.

4.

The four sentences to describe what you do and who you serve in your role (your pitch/ elevator speech) are:

1.

2.

3.

4.

After compiling this list, you will be able to incorporate these powerful words in your visual storyboard by creatively making sentences to be used as affirmations or using the individual words as visual cues to keep you accountable to what you say you want in your image and role. You can choose to make the words larger in a word processing document on your computer or handwrite the words to add to your visual storyboard.

These words will also be extremely useful when you are writing your marketing materials, talking to others about what you do, and assist you when making choices in your image. You can immediately refer to those words and see if you are visually displaying what it is you said you want to communicate to the world.

Tomorrow Ill show you how to add on the third component to your this visual storyboard.

Day 23

Whose Your
"Roles" Model ?

Role Model: A person who serves
as a model in a particular behavioral
or social role for another person to
emulate.

Whether you realize it or not, there are people that you see who you identify as someone whose style you admire their style. It could be their entire look, or elements of what they wear, sometimes even their posture that you admire. From a particular hair color, to a dress, to a rebel attitude, we are identifying with things that are signaling to us our actual preference for our look. Frustration comes when we don't know how to translate or identify what we like about them, and incorporate those elements into our finished look. So today we will take a look at what your "roles" model is, and begin to find pictures and descriptions of what it is you like about them that you can incorporate into your own role.

As you are creating and up leveling a visual brand that is your own, you can take clues from your roles models to add more insight to your visual story board.

Step 3: Identifying your roles model – Take this quiz to find out your roles style personality

Each one of us has a style that we gravitate towards – I like to call it our Roles Model for Style. Your roles model style personality is your innate tendency to choose a particular type of clothing. Most of the time the clothing choices that draw you are representative of your true self. While we sometimes make mistakes in articulating what we are drawn to, or simply make the wrong choices in combining elements of our roles style – once you are aware and can identify clearly what you like, it will become easier to communicate it purposely in your visual brand.

Even when we do see items we like, we can have a hard time choosing clothing because of the influences surrounding us or even familiarity through our upbringing, family, work atmosphere, social position, or the media. Unconsciously we make fashion decisions based off of other people's standards and expectations instead of knowing how to make the things we like our own in an appropriate manner.

Today I am going to help you find and evolve your own roles fashion style. When you become truly aware of what you like as well as how you are projecting yourself, you will begin to look at your entire closet differently. So let's begin!

Defining Your Roles Model for Style

Imagine you could create the perfect outfit. Your dream outfit consist of:

    a.   A staple white button-down shirt, a classic blazer, and a pair of basic skinny jeans and if dressy a little black dress

    b.   A motorcycle cropped leather jacket, chunky platform sandals, trendy earrings, studded clutch purse

    c.   Jumpsuit, statement necklace, sleek patent clutch purse, and your favorite stilettos

    d.   Tribal-inspired prints, eclectic jewels, beaded bracelet and easy shapes like maxi skirts and dresses.

    e.   A pretty dress, vintage-inspired purse, strappy sandals, simple stud earrings

    f.   Thrift store steal of a dress, bright-colored blazer, platform sandals, layers of necklace and an exotic clutch purse

Your personality is often a strong indicator of your fashion persona. Select the attributes that best describe your personality:

    a.   Well-groomed, sophisticated, organized

    b.   Rebel, trendsetter, spontaneous, confident

    c.   Independent, sexy, direct

    d.   Warm, southern comfort, laid back

    e.   Hopeless romantic, emotional, sensitive

    f.   Unconventional, artsy, creative

You can learn a lot about a person from their favorite colors. Believe it or not most people even know what colors look good on them because they feel a certain way when wearing them (i.e. powerful, creative, regal). What are your favorite colors?

    a.   I like playing it safe with neutrals, black, whites. I like monochromatic color combinations and I might throw in a subtle pop of color to keep it interesting

    b.   I like bold, fun and girlie colors such as pinks, orange and yellow. I love black in all kinds of textures as well as fun and trendy blocks color

    c.   I like colors that represent authority. I also dress for impact with one dress in a bold color such as purple or electric blue

    d.   I like simple, neutral colors as well as soft and delicate colors I'm also drawn to earthy colors.

    e.   I like girlie, delicate colors such as soft pinks, blues, and pastels.

    f.   I like mixing all kinds of colors and textures together. I love to express myself creatively and march to my own drum. I have a thing for bold, fun colors such as purple, electric blue and fuchsia. I also like rich, deep jewel toned colors.

While some people don't fully maximize the use of accessories, they can actually be very strong clues to your style influence. Accessories add interest and character to the wearer of the outfit, and can make or break an outfit. What type of accessories dominates your wardrobe?

    a.   Pearls, and stud earrings, classic multi-purpose necklaces and bracelets, as well as belts and pointed polished shoes

    b.   What's hot, that's what I'm wearing whether it's wedges or gladiator sandals. Trendy, statement jewelry and sunglasses; belts

    c.   Hoops, statement necklaces, oversized rings, signature designer handbags and shoes

    d.   Canvas, Converse sneakers and loafers, eco chic clothing, hobo handbags, natural stoned jewelry

e.   Vintage-inspired jewelry and necklaces, pretty purses, and flowing scarves

f.   Eclectic and fun statement accessories, statement hats, print scarves and bags – as well as layered necklaces and loads of bracelets

It's time to update your shoes and you head out on the quest to purchase your favorites. What type of shoes catches your eye?

a.   How many ways can I wear this shoe? Simple pumps, ballerina flats, riding boots. I like footwear in neutrals, but I will go out the box and try a colored shoe in red or blue.

b.   What's in for this season? I like edgy pieces, studs, and leather. I'll also wear designer sneakers like Pumas, or Adidas.

c.   How sexy can I make my leg look? I stay on stiletto watch, and like a strappy heel

d.   Comfort is the key and principle thing. So I like flats, comfy leather sandals and casual boots

e.   I want to feel pretty in my shoe. Vintage-inspired footwear like cute print flats, open toe pumps and wedge sandals

f.   I like to standout and be unique. Anything colorful, bold and signature will do. I love revisiting styles of the past like cowboy boots.

Where you shop says a lot about your roles style and fashion influence. If you were able to go on a shopping spree at your favorite stores, which ones would it be?

a.   Ann Taylor, Banana Republic, Nordstrom, The Gap, Dillard's

b.   Forever 21, Macy's, Lucky's, Guess

c.   BeBe, Bloomingdales, Net-a-porter, Cache

d.   Ralph Lauren, Old Navy, J.Crew, Steinmart

e.   Anthropologie, Victoria Secret

f.   Thrift shop, Consignment Shops, TJ Maxx, EBay

The inspiration we get for our outfits are usually influenced from fashion magazines, celebs and fashion icons. Which famous celebrity fashionistas would you say you look up to in terms of style?

    a.   First Lady Michelle Obama, Halle Berry, Kate Middleton, Keri Washington

    b.   Rihanna, Gwen Stefani, Pink

    c.   Jennifer Lopez, Beyoncé, Charlize Theron, Kim Kardashian

    d.   Zoe Saldana, Julianne Moore, Jennifer Anniston, Taylor Swift,

    e.   Eva Mendes, Angelina Jolie

    f.   Solange, Nicole Richie, Rachel Zoe, Zoe Kravitz

Whose hairstyle most represents the look you would like to project ?

    a.   The Chic Midlength style like: First Lady Michelle Obama, Diane Keaton, Nicole Ritchie, Cameron Diaz, Jennifer Anniston

    b.   The Short Cropped Mane like: Halle Berry, Charlize Theron, Michelle Williams , Anne Hathaway

    c.   Flowing Sexy Locks like: Beyoncé, Kim Kardashian, Catherine Zeta-Jones, Eva Mendes

    d.   A Natural Queen-Like Mane like: Jill Scott, Solange

I like makeup that is:

    a.   A signature look I can wear every day the same way

    b.   What ever is the trend, I like to explore it!

    c.   A smoky dramatic eye

    d.   Barely there makeup, maybe even bronze kissed skin

    e.   Old Hollywood glamour look, a strong color lipstick, and lots of lashes

    f.   Strong playful colors on my eyes that express the mood I'm in for the day

Calculate your answers

Now count how many A's, B's and so on you selected from each question.

If the result is a tie; or if you've scored highest on several questions – then look at these as your accent styles.

Mostly A's = The Sophisticated Classic
Mostly B's = The Trendy Rockstar
Mostly C's = The Dramatic Showstopper
Mostly D's =The Natural Bohemian
Mostly E's = The Hopeless Romantic
Mostly F's = The Artsy Creative

Day 24

Ready… Set … TAKE ACTION! Creating A Plan That Takes Action And Moves You Forward

Having a plan that creates change

So now that you understand more about your role, you are clearer when it comes to creating your visual brand, and you have your visual story-board to help you envision what your role looks like, all that's left is to do it! Now it's time for you to make concrete goals that will allow you to actualize your visual brand. One thing I know personally is that if you don't actually breakdown your goals into digestible and attainable assignments, they simply won't get done. You will have great intentions, but no system in which to get to your intended results.

What I am going to teach you here today legitimately revolutionized my life in the way that I approach getting things done. With so many things to do each day, it's easy to find yourself in the land of overwhelm, and end up on the street of "do nothing".

Here we will detail a step-by-step guide for creating an effective action plan – with a well-designed plan and daily action, you can achieve virtually any goal you set out to accomplish.

Step 1 – Know What You Want. Success comes by truly understanding a simple concept: If you don't decide where you're going in life, life will decide for you.

Step 2 – Be Specific About Your Goal. Not only must your goal be specific, but you must also create a specific intention as well as very specific tasks or steps that will move you toward the completion of that goal.

Step 3 – Create Measurable Milestones. Once you have a clear picture of what you're out to accomplish, as well as what targets you will need to hit throughout the time span of the project or period, the next step is to create measurable milestones. Create milestones easily by starting at the end in mind; what you actually want to accomplish and then work backwards and towards what it will take to reach the goal.

Step 4 – Create a List and a Time Line of specific action items or tasks to complete in order to hit those milestones.

Step 5 – Breakdown Large Tasks into Smaller, More Manageable Chunks. Some tasks or milestones may seem more daunting to achieve than others. That's when it makes sense to break larger tasks down into smaller, more manageable chunks.

Step 6 – Establish Time-lines for Everything. Without specific time frames and deadlines, work will definitely expand to fill the time allotted, and some tasks may never get completed.

Step 7 – Create a Visual Representation – Once you've created your action items and set a specific time-line, the next step is to create some type of visual representation of your plan. You might use a flowchart, sticky notes, or a spreadsheet. Attach your action list to your Visual Storyboard.

Step 8 – Schedule out Your Goals. Anyone relevant that is involved with a task should grab their schedule out their involvement.

Step 9 – Work Your Plan and Don't Stop Until it's Complete. Once your plan is established, shared with the team, and accomplishments are scheduled, the next step is simple: take daily action and follow up with responsible parties to ensure that everyone is doing their part.

Step 10 – Change the Date if You Must, but Never Give up on the Goal. Occasionally, circumstances or unforeseen events can arise that throw a wrench in your ability to meet deadlines, complete tasks and achieve your goal. If this happens, do not get discouraged – revise your plan and continue working to meet targets and move forward.

Step 11 – Celebrate Success. With each accomplishment, celebrate that you followed through and actually completed the task. You can choose to this monthly, quarterly, or a momentous celebration or reward in a year, the point is reward yourself for making the commitment and achieving your goals.

Step 4: Getting started with your Visual Branding Action Plan

Step 1 Set one clear goal in each one of your image quadrants:

1. Physical Image – makeup, hair, wardrobe
2. Body – weight management, exercise, nutrition, cleansing and detoxification
3. Marketing – headshots/promotional shots, website, online persona/social media, brochures, packaging
4. Mindset – your image assessment, dealing with image sabotagers, owning your role

Step 2 Identify your next progressive action steps for the next twelve weeks

Step 3 Put a start and end date with every goal, milestone, and action step. No matter what action items you choose for which phase of your action plan, it is essential that a time frame be attached to absolutely everything. Without follow-up, too many things can slip through the cracks and get missed. In some cases, missing just one milestone can be enough to set your entire project behind, which means missing the mark for your goal. Regular follow-up is essential in order to prevent this.

Example:

Your Goal
    Milestone #1
        Action Step 1
        Action Step 2
        Action Step 3

Milestone #2
    Action Step 1
    Action Step 2
    Action Step 3

Day 25

Understanding Your Body Shape: Apples, Pears, Rectangles, and an Hourglass

All About Your Body Shape

It's the reason why you like one pair of jeans over the other. The reason why you have a favorite "works like a charm" dress. The reason why you buy a particular designer for your slacks because they just "feel good on". The one thing that all three have in common is the way the items look on your body. But what would happen if all of your clothes looked great on you? In fact, what if the mystery was taken out of why one item of clothing works better than the other? Today we are talking about understanding your body shape; a subject that once understood and mastered will revolutionize your wardrobe. Whether you like your body figure or not – if you understand your current body shape, and the basic style guidelines for enhancement – you can wear clothes in a way that boosts your self-esteem and flatters your figure. When you begin to train your eye to hone in on the items that fit the shape of your body, shopping gets simpler and you can make every outfit a hit!

While your size can change in clothing the basic makeup of your body also known as your frame remains the same. Your goal should then be to create balance with your body so that it looks as proportioned as possible.

Brandi's 6 Rules to Maximizing Your Body Shape

Rule #1: Discover your body shape and then let the shape guide EVERY clothing purchase!

Your body shape is the overall silhouette of your body. Your body shape is determined by how the contours of your body figure and how your upper, mid and lower half are in proportion with each other.

How to Determine Your Body Shape
Step a few feet away from a full-length mirror and observe your overall body shape. Pay attention to the relationship between all of your body parts from your bust, waist, hips, and the length and shape of your legs.

Stand up straight and measure each part of your body to include:

- Shoulder to shoulder
- Your bust: underneath your arms, around the fullest part of your chest
- Smallest part of your waist
- Low waist: one inch down from your natural waist
- Hips: 6-9 inches from your natural waist
- Thigh: at it's widest part

Another trick is to measure the widest point of your shoulders and hips, and the thinnest part of your waist. For example an hourglass is always between 8" to 10" smaller than the hip or bust measurement

After analyzing your shape take a look below to see where your body shape fits

The 5 Body Shapes

The Hourglass: Torso and hips are approximately the same width – with waist definition

Your #1 Thing to remember: Your waist is your focal point. Wearing clothing or accessories that wraps snugly around the thinnest part of your waist or draws attention to this body part can really bring out your perfect proportions.

Famous Hourglass: Halle Berry, Megan Fox, Salma Hayek, Scarlett Johansson, Jessica Biel, Marilyn Monroe

The Pear: Torso and upper body are *smaller* than your hips with waist definition

Your #1 Thing to remember: Add dimensions to your upper body to create balance. Wear anything that visually adds more weight to your shoulder and bust area and brings attention to your upper body. This makes your body figure look more proportional like an Hourglass, as well as de-emphasizing your hips and thighs.

Famous Pears: Beyoncé, Jennifer Lopez, Rihanna, Kristen Davis

Inverted triangle: Torso and upper body *wider* than your hips – with little waist definition
Your #1 thing to remember: Adding more volume and width around your hip-line and thighs downplays your broad shoulders and balances out your silhouette.

Famous Inverted Triangles: Naomi Campbell, Demi Moore, Giselle Bundchen

Rectangle: Torso and upper body are the *same width* as your hips – little waist definition
Your #1 thing to remember: Add Dimensions to Your Body Frame. This means "breaking up" your silhouette to create curves from waist up and waist down.

Famous Rectangles: Cameron Diaz, Nicole Kidman, Rachel Hunter

Apple: Torso and upper body *wider* than your hips – with little or no waist definition. You might have weight surrounding your waist.
Your #1 Thing to remember: Trim your waist. Your abdominal and torso are in general your biggest body issues, so you'll need to focus on de-emphasizing this area as well as accentuate your best parts. In many cases of apple shapes, these parts are your breasts and legs.

Famous Apples: Oprah Winfrey, Catherine Zeta-Jones, Angelina Jolie

Rule #2: Look at Your Body Figure as a Whole

It's all about balance and your body proportions. The goal is to focus on achieving a proportional and balanced body silhouette like that of an hourglass and to camouflage your "problem areas" or prominent body areas (i.e. belly and thighs). The key is to highlight your best assets, and play down the others. When you look at your outfit as a complete look, you will pay attention to how each piece complements the other.

Rule #3: Pay Attention To the Fit of Your Clothing

Good fitting clothing will skim, not hijack the outline of your shape. Your clothing should not cling or pull, or be so oversized that it hides your body's silhouette. That's why your clothing will look best when it's bought with your specific shape and needs in mind.

Whenever I try on clothing I always look at it on my body at all angles: from the front, back, and side profile. There should be no gapping, pulling, sagging, or puckering anywhere along the outfit.

Key Areas to look at for fit:

- Around your armholes
- Across your bust
- Across your stomach
- Across your sleeves and shoulders, especially the widest part of your arm
- Where your buttons close
- The length range of your arm
- Across your behind and crotch
- Through your thigh area

Rule #4: Wear fabric that flatters

Pay close attention to the surface quality of fabric, some fabrics that add texture to a garment can also add unwanted volume to your frame. Clothing with a matte finish can be more figure flattering then shiny clothing. Fabrics like matte stretch fabrics and Lycra help to mold, shape, and hug your curves and can be very flattering. Other flattering fabrics are jersey, cashmere, fine cotton, spandex, flat knits, matte crepe silk, and wool rayon.

Rule #5 If you don't like something, work on it, but don't beat yourself up, and rock your RIGHT NOW shape!

Determine that you will be you at your best today, and that means well-dressed for your body as it is now – not twenty pounds from now, six months of Boot camp from now, or a juice fast away, but right now – life's opportunities won't wait, rock the best you now.

Rule #6 Don't get hung up on the size, buy clothing for the right fit

I know people that will continue to buy the wrong size, even though it does not fit, out of habit or denial. Some will even refuse to buy clothing until they are a particular size – the size being the key factor. I'll have to admit, I myself have a certain range in size that when I reach it I know it's time to push away from the table. Throughout the years however, that size has changed as the proportions of my body shifts, so now I pay more attention to the way the clothing fits as opposed to having to wear a particular size. Your philosophy is your own, and I certainly don't want to discourage you from maintaining a healthy weight.

What I have found to be true however is that when you dismiss size and get what looks good on you, although you may not like the number, there's also freedom that comes with wearing items that fit well.

Often times stylists tailor many of the clothing items to specifically fit the client, which is why items look like they were made for the person. But guess what, you can do the same thing! So the next time you are choosing between the size 10 and 12, but the 12 fits better, just know to go for the fit instead of the size.

Another thing to consider is the actual designer, because all sizes are not created or cut equal so your size 8 in one dress could be a size 6 in another line. I'll never forget the day my Mom showed me the size changes that have occurred over the years as we as a country have been upsized. My Mom showed me a size 8 vintage dress that would actually by all standards today be a size 4/6. As we have become larger, the designers want us to still feel good about ourselves, so they have changed the sizes drastically from that of yesteryear. My point? Get what fits, and if you don't like the size, work on it, but again, rock your role now!

Enlisting a tailor

With a little tailoring you can make every outfit a work of art on your shape. A great tailor will make your clothing look beautiful from any angle. When you've found the right one, the return is priceless.

Suggestions for finding a tailor:

- Seek out referrals from your friends.
- The colleague whose clothing always looks so good on them may be another resource who has a tailor behind the scenes doing subtle nips and tucks in just the right places.
- Look on the internet for custom tailoring in your area
- Some department stores offer free tailoring services with purchase
- Dry cleaners
- Bridal salons

If you find that the dry cleaner or bridal salon sends their work out to be tailored see if you can contact the person direct to service you.

When establishing a relationship with a tailor start with a smaller task first to see their work – like a hem or taking a garment in at the waist. When you get the item back, check for the uniformity of the work, stitching, and if your garment lays smooth with no bunching (especially if it has a lining). The best way to make sure you get your desired outcome is to consult with the tailor first to have clear understanding of what needs to be done. Allow them to make suggestions to improve the piece, and bring pictures where necessary to help illustrate what you want the outcome to be.

Exploring What Lies Beneath

When you see women walking the red carpet or performing on stage, it seems as if the clothing fits perfectly on their body, no matter the size. The secret to flattering clothes lies in the fit and fabric, but also in what lies beneath the clothing providing support and structure to the garment and wearer. I knew that this discussion was one that had to be highlighted because so many women underestimate the power of what they wear underneath their clothes. The proper fitting bra, and slimming accessories has the ability to make the garment look better, cause slimming where necessary, and bring the illusion that we didn't consume that extra bit of popcorn last night at the movies!

Be Bra-wildered No More!

Bras: having the right fit and shape.
Let's face it; most women look at their bras as just the right thing to do and a means of strapping down the girls. However, one of the most important items in every woman's wardrobe is her bra. The right, or wrong, bra can entirely change the look and feel of the rest of an outfit. The right bra promotes comfort and a great look instead of a strained back and

shoulders. The right bra can give you the needed lift most ladies need if they are anywhere over 30 (and sometimes even younger).

One of the biggest problems with being *bra-wildered* is we simply don't know what bra is right for us, in fact 85% of women are wearing the wrong sized bra. The best gift a woman can give to herself is a bra fitting by a well trained fitter that can measure and size you quickly and accurately in the lingerie departments of most fine department stores or specialty stores like Intimacy.

A typical fitting begins with measuring and then moves to your specialist bringing in several recommendations for your determined size, body type and of course your wardrobe needs. It ends, usually, with you no longer being bra-wildered and moving into a new found freedom. You will quickly see how your clothes look completely different due to the fit of the bra.

You should be fitted for a bra about every six months, or whenever there have been changes to your body, such as weight change or pregnancy.

If you want to attempt to measure yourself at home, take a shot! Follow this standard formula used by stores and manufacturers alike.

How to measure your bra size
Braless, and in your underwear, hold your tape measure directly under your bust and measure around your chest. This number determines your band size.

- If the number is odd, and 5
- If the numbers even, at 6
- If the numbers over 33 inches, and 3

Next, hold your tape around the fullest part of your breasts to measure your cup size. Subtract your band size from your cup size, and if the difference is:

- 0 = AA
- 1 = A
- 2 = B
- 3 = C
- 4 = D
- 5 = DD
- 6 = DDD

When you try on a bra

Lean forward and place your breasts into the cups, push them from the side to the center of the cup and hook the back. Adjust the straps so that your breasts are centered and the line looks natural.

How you know to put the bra back:

1. Your breasts spill over the sides: You know you need to increase your band and/or cup size
2. The cups wrinkle or pucker: Try different style or smaller cup. Try a demi cup rather than a fuller-cup cut for better fit and a natural-looking shape.
3. The bra rides up in the back: The band is probably too large. Any band should cross the center of your back and stay there to fit securely. Try a smaller band size.
4. It gaps at the top of the cup or the underwire is not flushed to your rib cage.
5. Your two breasts are pushed together into one sausage-shaped breast. Don't wear your sports bra under your clothing if you want a sleek look. Try an underwire for more definition.

Smoothing it out

Shape wear and other illusions

Great shaping garments can whittle your entire body down a size and provide support and lift at your rear so that you look like you've been doing squats and abs exercises. Shape wear comes in pieces that can smooth you out from head to toe. When selecting any shape wear it should move with your body. This means it should not ride up, not squeeze you, not pinch you or create rolls at any openings. If you can barely breath while wearing the garment, that's a clear indication that it's not the correct size for you. Once on, you should not have to constantly pull on it, you should feel supported but not self-conscious. So let's take a look at some some shapers that work.

Lower Body Shapers
Spanx – mid calf, mid-thigh, high-waisted and footless options for light-weight control from the waist to below the knee
Assets – Spanxs product line sold at Target
Bali – body by Bali briefs and thigh slimmers
Hanes – body enhancers
Victoria's Secret – foot less control top
Walmart – Sweet Nothings – Get the Skinny Shapers

Body Suits
Wacoal – Seamless control bodysuit in cups up to DD
Bali – Body by Bali Concealers with seamless, convertible bra straps
Flexees – Control wear

All Over Coverage
The unitard is a longtime favorite of professionals because it provides flawless, line-free shaping. A favorite amongst curvy entertainers, the lightweight unitards are a line-free solution that moves with the body and enhances the illusion of a well-toned body.

Body Wrap – Seamless, Firm Control Unitard
Nancy Ganz – Firm Control Unitard, Body Shaping Unitard

Bra slips
Lane Bryant – Cacique Body Slip
Body Wrap – Bra slip
Flexees – Body slip that doesn't ride up when you walk

Day 26

Get To The Core Of Your Closet: Creating a Core Wardrobe Plan

Creating a Core Wardrobe Plan

Do you find yourself having lots of clothes in the closet but nothing to wear? When an event comes up, do you feel like you have to go out and purchase something in an emergency shopping sprint? You are not alone, most people's closets are filled with clothing that doesn't serve them or flatter.

We wear about 20% of what's in out closet 80% of the time.

What every person should have in their wardrobe as it's core boils down to a handful of basics. The key in working the basics is that they fit your roles personality, and your personal style. By narrowing your focus when shopping for your core wardrobe, you'll find that you make better decisions when it comes down to getting a wardrobe that really works for you. The goal is to build a wardrobe in such a way that when you look in the closet you see nothing but wins and endless combinations of clothing to produce star worthy outfits.

Earlier in the book I showed you how to determine your shape and understand the clothing that would be flattering on your frame. Along with understanding your shape, now we are going to create what I call your Core Wardrobe Plan. A Core Wardrobe Plan helps you to create the foundation for wardrobe success by knowing what to look for to build a dream wardrobe.

I like to help my clients create a wardrobe that mimics how they pack when they are going on a great trip. When you go on a great trip, you usually get clothing that is comfortable for you, works for every event that you attend, and is multi-purposed. The clothing is also very flattering, and the items that are packed for the trip make you feel most like yourself, even if you're away from home.

Now Rome wasn't built in a day, and neither will your wardrobe. Nobody can assemble a perfect wardrobe in a day or even a week unless it's me (smile), or your hired professional (me, again!). It's a process. Personally when I'm looking to up-level my image, I am constantly looking at magazines and movies for inspiration, and look to my "role" models; allowing myself the freedom to incorporate a bit of "role" appropriate trends to add to my classic pieces.

Now that you know your body shape, it's also going to be easier to create your core wardrobe now that you understand what to buy that will be flattering to you. It will also help you to no longer repeat the old shopping patterns you displayed before coming into the knowledge of dressing for your shape and role.

So let's begin!

In this section, I outline the ingredients for my 40 Core Wardrobe Plan. These are the basics and create endless options for you because they can be mixed and matched repeatedly.

The 40 Core Wardrobe Plan

Six shirts

3 button-down shirts (make one neutral-black or gray, white or cream, brown or tan)
3 blouses

Button up shirts: Some pieces are just classics, and can transition form one era to another. The collared white shirt looks great on just about everyone. The white button-down shirt should fit you well. At first glance, your white shirt may look no different than the one your husband or boyfriend wears under his suits, but yours is made and cut specifically for a woman. It should be flattering and accentuate your best features. You can wear a white shirt on its own, tucked in or out, under a sweater, under a jacket, or as part of a suit.

To add color to an otherwise neutral suit try a colored shirt that when paired with a colored shoe adds a fashion forward element to any work-centered ensemble.

Four stylish tees
>   2 short or long sleeve
>   2 tanks

Tank tops and tees can serve multiple purposes. You have your neutral colored tank tops that can be paired with jeans or under a blazer, and then you have stylish statement shirts that either support a cause, or add character. These shirts can also be paired with jeans, be worn under blazers or with a statement necklace as well.

Six sweaters
>   3 neutral sweaters
>   3 colorful sweaters

Six pants
>   3 trousers
>   3 jeans (one of each for play, date night, work)

A great fitting pant is worth its weight in gold! This is where truly understanding your body shape completely pays off. Stay away from pleats because they only accentuate an area that no one really needs accentuating! If you can buy only one pair of trousers, select a length that matches the heel height you most commonly wear. And choose lightweight wool that will work in summer or winter. When talking about jeans, a dark wash is the most versatile with deep blue and black being extremely flattering: not to mention appropriate for any age. You can wear them totally casual during the day, and you can dress them up for night.

Three skirts
    2 pencils or A – line skirts
    1 full/long skirt or short skirt

The basic black skirt and sweater set — always chic and classic. Every woman should have a knee-length black skirt that fits perfectly and gives her a slim appearance. The particular style is up to you (and what looks good on your body type): It can be a pencil skirt or an A-line skirt. So that it can go from sea- son to season, look for one that's light-weight wool.

Six dresses
    4 work/day dresses
    1 little black dress
    1 colorful cocktail dress

The LBD – Little Black Dress: Ah, the little black dress. It should be sexy, yet sophisticated. It should be well made and fit like a glove. It should hide your flaws and accentuate your attributes. It can go from day (wear it to the office with a cardigan or blazer and a set of pearls and leather pumps) to night (take off the blazer or cardigan and add some makeup, jewelry, and heels). Choose a LBD in the style that suits you, makes you feel comfortable, and looks most like *you*. It can be sleeveless, have cap sleeves, or have 3/4-length sleeves. It can have a V-neck, boat neck, crew neck, or square neck. It can be knee-length, a little longer, a little shorter, or miniskirt length. The LBD is both universal and individual at the same time. Find one that makes you feel fabulous and make the investment because this is one piece that really gives you your money's worth!

Three suits (with pants or skirt)
    1 black
    1 other neutral tone
    1 color

Six coats
>   1 trench
>   3 fitted Blazer
>   1 three-quarter length
>   1 Stylish Leather Jacket

Blazer: A well-cut jacket is a great layering piece plus it can pull any outfit together and make it look more polished. A great blazer looks just as good with the white tee as it does with skinny jeans for daytime, or with the great pair of slacks. The black blazer is key in your wardrobe. Because it's black, it goes with virtually everything. You can change the look just by changing the accessories. Although it doesn't need to be ridiculously expensive or high-end, the blazer does need to fit you perfectly and work with your body type.

Bonus Item: A great shaper: A great mid-thigh or mid-calf shaper will help to eliminate visible panty lines and firm up your behind under skirts, dresses and in slacks. If you want to slim down your midsection as well, opt for the high-waist shaper to cinch the waist especially when wearing fitted dresses. A smoothing cami also goes a long way to flatten out back rolls and bra lines. For those who want "maximum" suck-in, there are also high-compression bodysuits for those extra special events where you are looking to shrink a size to look extra special in your dress.

The 40 Core Accessories

Ten shoes
>   3 heels (black, 2 colorful)
>   3 flats (neutral)
>   2 boots (1 heeled, 1 flat)
>   1 stylish sneaker
>   1 cross trainer sneaker

Seven bags

  2 neutrals (make one of them black or brown)
  2 colors
  1 tote
  1 evening bag
  1 stylish workbag

About Handbags: When choosing a bag think about the bag's main functions. Do you need it to make a powerful statement; you might consider a higher price investment bag. Do you always have to carry a lot around; a hobo bag might work better. Do you need a bag to only carry the basics; you may need a small but impactful clutch. Do you wear a lot of dark clothing and need to use your bag to add color? Thinking about your day-to-day and special events in life will allow you to make better choices when deciding on a handbag.

Three belts (make one of them neutral)

  1 medium-width belt
  1 narrow belt
  1 wide belt

Jewelry

  2 pairs chandelier earrings
  2 hoops
  2 pairs stud earrings (pearl, diamond/Cubic Zirconia, gold/silver)
  3 statement piece necklaces
  2 short necklaces
  2 long necklaces
  2 bangles and/or cuffs
  2 watches (one leather band, one link)
  3 cocktail rings

The Statement Piece: Your statement piece is an eye-catching element of your outfit. They usually reflect the personality of the wearer and come in the form of accessories: bangles, rings, earrings, scarfs, and purses. Add a statement necklace to a sheath dress that has a simple neckline to instantly transform it from business to evening chic.

Bonus Items: Colored Scarfs

I love scarfs because they are one of the easiest ways to add color, texture, and pizzazz to an outfit. It can serve the same purpose as a statement necklace, but is also doubles to keep you warm and comfortable as well. I love to use scarves with my clients because it's a great way to accessorize without breaking the bank. You can opt to get a rainbow of solid scarfs or you can go for some that are printed.

Day 27

Clarity is King! Purging, Releasing & Repurposing Your Wardrobe

Get rid of what doesn't serve your role and repurpose what does

Detoxing Your Closet to Make Room For a True "Role" Wardrobe

This is an area that most of us will admit we don't want to address but we have to; mastering our closets. I say we because I am in this journey with you guys! Before we can go shopping for new clothing we have to first see what's inside the closet that matches your current role, and purge what does not.

Many women tell me that their closets are stuffed to capacity, and it makes it difficult to make choices in terms of outfits because they become overwhelmed with facing the clutter. What I've found is the more organized my closet is, the more I can truly see the clothing that I want to wear.

Even after organizing your closet, to keep it in tiptop shape I suggest reevaluating the contents every six months. With everything having a place to go, you can easily identify if something is out of place and put it back in it's proper place.

What you will need:

- At least half a day or one hour per day through a dedicated week
- A clothing rack if you have one or an empty bed
- A full length mirror, along with a hand held mirror so you can see yourself from all angles
- Giant trash bags and shopping bags
- Patience, some good music, and energy snacks
- A good friend if you wish to join in the fun!

As you sort through your clothing, create the following 7 piles (these can also be immediately put in labeled bags) After reviewing your items, you will likely end up with all or most of these categories:

- **Keep** – clothing, shoes, and accessories that fit and flatter you

- **Trash** – torn or stained items that are unwearable
- **Give to Friends** – items you would like someone special to have
- **Donations** – for charity
- **Alterations & Repairs** – items that can be worn again with a little help
- **Seasonal** – items that need to be stored for another season
- **Consignment/Garage Sale** – items you'd like to sell instead of donate

Brandi's 5 Step Closet Detox

STEP 1 – Identify what's in your closet that fits your roles and fits you properly

STEP 2 – Purge & Release what does not – immediately

STEP 3 – Repurpose what fits your roles and body shape

STEP 4 – Put in action an immediate plan to take clothing to be donated, sell, given to someone special, or tailored

STEP 5 – Plan for shopping to get additional items you need based on my Core Wardrobe Plan

Pick up any clothing on the floor and get laundry started while you work. The first order of business is to tidy up in your room and closet as much as possible.

Make a pledge to be realistic and honest with yourself. Avoid the traps of keeping things that are too large or small, out of style, or unflattering in fit or color.

Try every single thing on. Take out every single thing in your closet and move it all to a corner of the room. Make sure you have room for a clear workspace and for multiple bags. I suggest to try everything on because we all have clothes that never see the light of day because they…

- Don't fit
- Are not stylish
- Need tailoring
- Are long forgotten because we can't see them

Also….

- If you try on something that's fits poorly or is unflattering, put it in a bag, which is destined for a visit to the tailors.

- If you find something that does not match your current role or the role you inspire to hold, or does not fit your body shape that we've already defined, put it in the bag to donate or give to friend bag (depending on the quality)

- If you try on something and realize you haven't worn in at least 1 year, it means it's probably not a priority you have 2 choices: if it's a high quality piece and fits into your role, it can go back in the closet if you promise to create outfits around the piece, or #2 donate

- If you try on something and are over it at first glance, put it in bag to donate

- If you try on anything that is stained or ripped beyond repair, it goes in the trash bag.

- If you try on something that is two sizes to big or too small it goes to donate, you can always buy something in the correct size when you've lost weight or gotten to your desired size

- If the try on something and it does not look great on you but will be perfect on someone else, place it in the bag under give to a friend, or donate, if it's really nice, consider selling on eBay.

- If you try on something from several years ago and are keeping it because you know the style is going to come back a round, put it in the donate bag (when the style comes back around, you can buy a new version)

- Sort through shoes, and accessories. Be sure to have your core wardrobe plan with you to make note of items to buy to complete the project, and new wardrobe items that you need to purchase.

- If you find something that›s a clear winner, it›s has earned a place back in your closet

I know, I know it's so hard to say good-bye – even to clothes you are not wearing. We become attached to what we wear. But when you continue to hold on to clothing that's not representing the role that you are currently in or positioning you for where you are going, you allow those clothes to take space away from clothing that could be on it's way. It's better to have ten great items that work every time, then 50 that are questionable and taking up space.

What to do next

Make a promise to yourself to get rid of the purged clothes immediately. The reason why is that if you don't remove the clothes immediately, you can easily find yourself slipping back into the bags to wear the item "one last time". Before you know it, half the bag is back in your closet. Another reason for immediately taking action and dispersing the clothes is the clutter it will take up in your house. We are trying to simply your life, so you want to finish your closet detox by closing the chapter on the session completely.

Plan a shopping trip

- Establish a Budget and a timeline for building your wardrobe

- Establish what you need most and prioritize
- See where the sales may be on your items of choice
- Utilize online as well as brick and mortar stores
- Don't be afraid to ask for help where you need it.

Create a "look book" of go to's useable at any time. Once you find outfits that work every time, create your own look book of styles you can always count on to work no matter the occasion. You can also incorporate ideas here from online stores or take pictures of complete outfits in stores as well to put on your visual storyboard. If you have weight release goals, this is a great place to put your new looks for inspiration.

Sort the clothing you're keeping by season, then by type, sleeve length, and color. Think of it as "filing" your clothes and you need to determine the way in which you will sort. Some people may prefer sorting by casual, career, and formal clothing as well. People in warmer climates may not need to sort by season. The more organized your clothing is, the more delight you will have in getting dressed.

Usage determines storage. Prioritize placement of your items by the frequency of their use. If you use it often, make it more accessible.

Consider purchasing new hangers. This is a "secret" of professional organizers. I love the huggable hangers found almost anywhere; they allow for clothing to stay securely on the hangers and come in a variety of colors. This one change can make a significant difference in the way your closet looks and feels.

Find a way to easily see and select all accessories. I have sorted my accessories in many ways over the years, but the main thing is that you can see all of your pieces so you have the ability to easily choose pieces that match your ensemble. Whether it is to hang pieces on the walls, individual containers, multi-tiered displays, the key is visibility. We won't wear what we can't see, and will end up wearing the same pieces out of habit.

Day 28

Feel as Good As You Look: Exercising, Nutrition, and Releasing the Weight

The busier life became, and the more I stepped into my role, the more I realized the need to be healthy across the board. I realized there were certain things that were non-negotiable when it comes to health, and that making healthy choices were now a lifestyle- not a fad, or a quick fix; a lifestyle. I realized that to be able to perform at top speed, I would have to put the right fuel in the tank!

There is a formula for good health, and it requires balance.
The formula is:
Exercise + Good Nutrition + Water + Detox + Rest = Good Health.

This formula requires putting you first and committing to treat your body well. In the long run it helps you to be around for all of the precious moments in your families life, and allows you to fully enjoy the fruits of your labor.

This formula also means that you will sometimes have to say no to things that don't work inside of your schedule, diet, and regimen you put in place to be healthy. And of course it requires a lot of discipline.

The one thing that I began to realize was that my productivity in work was directly influenced by how disciplined I was with my health. When I was extremely clear, and very creative, it usually was in direct correlation to eating clean, detoxing, and exercising.

In a society where the majority of the population is overweight, we are so busy that we rush to prepare food for our families, and too tired for exercise, it sometimes feels like an ongoing battle; a Ferris wheel we can't seem to get off of.

I spent much of my life dieting. The journey started at about 12 years old; that was when I realized that I had the power to change the way that I look through exercising and through eating differently. I could write an entire book on this journey (hmm, maybe I will!). Of course, much like other teenage girls, my sudden awareness of being overweight came as a result of becoming a teenager, being interested in boys, and recognizing after being told over and over again that I was overweight. Now some hundreds of pounds both lost and gained, I have recognized what I believe to be my truth, my philosophy that I choose to live with and practice as a lifestyle. Good health allows you to be able to fulfill the purpose of your life. What I found was that balance in health seemed to consist of 8 pillars that I have identified as key to all good health, and I have observed from others to be successful – so I 'll share what I've learned with you!

My Eight Health Pillars

Pillar 1: Eat for Life. Let me first say that I love good food, I love cooking, and I love celebrating with food. For this reason, I had to learn how to cook foods I love in a healthier way and control my portions. I also discovered that all of the fast food items that we like were much more healthier and fulfilling when I cooked them at home. One of my favorites is making homemade pizza with my son. It's a great way to have family time as well as create a family favorite without all of the calories.

Pillar 2: Move Your body – Make the world your gym! – In the words of my husband and Fitness trainer Curtis Mitchell, there are no excuses, you can turn anything into a workout, and create a good sweat no matter where you are. Developing a work out regimen benefits your heart, relieves stress, keeps us mobile as we age, and provides a good example for our children. Find ways to burn calories doing what you love, and it won't feel like exercise. One of my favorites is climbing Stone Mountain here in Georgia! It gives me the absolute most accomplishing feeling to look over the city and know that I climbed my way to the top to enjoy that view! Keep in mind that you have to constantly challenge yourself, which is why you have to track your progress with what you are doing, or have a trainer. Why? Because a good trainer will push you past what you could ever do for yourself. You may think the routine you are doing on your own is great until you realize you are not seeing any results or the same results as when you started. That's because the body has excellent memory, and will simply stop responding to what you do because it becomes used to it. You got to shake it up a bit.

Pillar 3: Cleanse & Detox – Where do I start with this... there are so many benefits to detoxing. When you think about all the different foods that we eat and the toxins we consume on a day-to-day basis, we all at some point have to detox and pull away and purge out the things that we actually consume. For me cleansing and detox means raw vegetables, fresh juices, and cleansing of the colon every season.

A detox aims to get rid of food-related toxins--like those found in alcohol, sugars and some fats--which have been linked to a whole host of problems: exhaustion, digestive ailments and depression, and being overweight. Some benefits said to come from detoxing are: radiant completion, weight release, decrease in headaches, clarity, energy, break of sugar/starch addictions, and other health related benefits.

Pillar 4: Juicing. Awwh... Juicing... I was first introduced to juicing from a client of mine who was 50 but had the energy and body of someone who was 30. I admired her energy level and her ability to be so productive through a busy day and still have energy to exercise and run around with her grandchildren. I watched as she would come into our sessions with a refrigerated bag full of raw juices and healthy snacks. At the time I thought her health lifestyle was so far away from what I was currently doing, until I tried one of her juices and the rest is history! Now I enjoy fresh juices every day. My favorite juices always contain a collection of greens that include cucumber and ginger. I have gone on to introduce many of my clients to juicing who have now chosen to incorporate it into their lives as well because they feel the benefits on so many levels. When I travel, if I don't have access to a juicer, I'll go to Whole Foods or a local Juice Bar where they can make fresh juices for you. When I'm in meetings and every one is eating pastries and salted goods,

I sip on a blended meal chock full of vitamins that will provide me with consistent energy throughout the day.

Pillar 5: Eat Fruits & Veggies Daily – I discovered that green vegetables were my friends! Thermo genic vegetables burn more calories then their caloric value so they actually work with you when you are attempting any weight release program. Even on cheat days, say if I decide to have pizza, I always try my best to have a big salad to go along with it because I know that it's going to fill me up so that I can't eat as much pizza. Fruits are great because they can fulfill that sugar fix you need and are good for you as well.

Pillar 6: Allow Cheat Meals Occasionally – Many successful weight release programs have a cheat meal as a common factor. So basically you eat to live all week, and one day out the week you *love* to eat! What this does is starve off cravings and also fool your body into releasing weight because if you've been eating clean all week, the shift in eating somehow helps you to release weight. Now this is all in moderation, and really should be a cheat meal, not an entire day. But take note; if you are on a regimen where you are really trying to break sugar addiction or carbs, you have to use your judgment in indulging in a cheat meal that contains either. You don't want to sabotage yourself and turn a cheat day into a cheat week, to turn into a cheat month!

Pillar 7: Drink H2O – They say that by the time you feel thirsty you may be dehydrated. The average person should consume 8 to 10 glasses minimum. Besides helping you to have more energy and flushing out toxins, water has so many benefits I had to take the time out to share just a fraction of them with you.

A Few Benefits of Water

1. **External benefits:** additional moisture for our skin prevents the aging process, a more fit body, etc.

2. **Headaches:** 75% of our brain is made of water. So, when the body has a water deficit, the brain will be the one of the first who will signal the problem, causing headaches.

3. **Back pains:** are often caused by fluid deficits in our bodies. The disks within our backs are filled with fluids, mainly water, and act like shock absorbers.

4. **Reduces infections:** the lymphatic systems in our body are responsible for waste disposal. This system breaks down toxins before passing them into the blood stream.

5. **Concentration:** water is used to flush out toxins contained by certain food products (preservatives, additives, etc.). By drinking water, these toxins are flushed quickly from the liver, making you more active and increasing your concentration capacity.

6. **Arthritis:** water is used to lubricate joints between our bones. When water intake is low, the friction between cartilage surfaces increases, causing swellings, pains, etc.

7. **Breath:** bad breath is a clear sign that your body needs more water. Our saliva helps the cleaning process of our teeth of bacteria and keeps our tongue hydrated.

8. **Cramps:** oxygen is transported to our muscles by blood. If the blood is not properly oxygenated, muscles create lactic acid causing cramps. By drinking water we make sure that our blood is fueled with oxygen.

9. **Other important benefits:** helps with asthma, digestion, fluid retention, morning sickness, etc.

10. **There are many other benefits of drinking water.** A proper hydrated body is a more healthy and resistant body!!!

Pillar 8: Plan Ahead Always – You are always going to have a business meeting with goodies, and stopping at a fast food will seem like the quickest fix for hunger. In order to maintain a healthy lifestyle it requires preparation and having balance, so you have to learn how to make better choices and prepare ahead. Some ways to prepare are by bringing your snacks with you, looking ahead at menus so you make a good choice, and snack through the day every 2-3 hrs. so that you won't pounce on the food when you finally eat. I try to keep spare apples, tuna fish kits, and baggies of protein around at all times.

The 8 Pillars and how they work in releasing weight

Have you ever lost 20 pounds? And did you find it again? Or did it find you? Well, "**releasing weight**" is just that, you release it, so **it never finds you again**. There are many reasons why we gain weight, keep weight on, or use weight as a coping tool.

Just think about times that you have committed, for an amount of time, to "lose" the weight. The problem comes in however when we don't create a way to deal with the reasons why the weight returns.

Perhaps your weight has been protection from unwanted attention. Maybe eating has been a way of coping with stress or anxiety. Some people use food to manage or suppress emotions. Whatever the reason – your behavior around food has served some purpose. You have used food to meet some need.

95% of weight management programs DON'T work because they fail to address the underlying cause of eating patterns, and in turn you fail to maintain what you have "lost". So the goal is to not only to release the weight, but also to incorporate a lifestyle that enables you to maintain the new you – maintaining commands true disciple.

Benefits of being at your ideal weight:

- Clarity
- Feeling Light
- Save money on clothing
- Boosts of confidence
- Save time – things fit better, and you have more options
- Consistency keeps you always ready for events
- Can incorporate exercise and healthy cooking into family time
- Relieves Stress
- Less Guilt
- Ward off inheritable diseases that are associated with weight
- MORE ENERGY!

So should you be on the road to truly releasing the weight, just remember....

It takes 21 days to break a habit or create a new one...
So when deciding on changing your body and mastering the 8 pillars, make your first goal to stick it out for at least 3 weeks so that what you are introducing to your body gets the time to adapt, and the old habits have a chance to quiet down and come under control. Often times we quit just before our body begins to respond, so be patient with yourself, but CHOOSE to honor your body by treating it good!

Have a recovery plan dictated by high stressed events or celebratory happenings in your life.
Look ahead at your calendar and realize when you will have heavy eating months (like the holidays, vacations, large events) and plan a recovery strategy ahead of time to get back on track.

Always take workout DVDs or consider going virtual with your trainer while traveling

My husband Curtis now trains people all across the globe in a boot camp class where people get great results all in the comfort of their own home and in front of the computer. Learn more at www.getfitwithcurtis.com

Day 29

All About Hair:
Enhancing Your Hair
by Incorporating the
3 C's Formula

Operation Honey Blonde

My first true experiment with hair was between me and a bottle of honey blonde hair color. My Mom always did my Grandmothers hair every Saturday morning, and then my Grandma would visit for the rest of the day. My Grandmother had jet-black hair, but this Saturday morning she decided she wanted to go honey blonde. The look only lasted about a month, but for me, I saw the color and fell in love! It was going to me and that honey blonde box of hair color against the world. I made up in my mind that I needed to add a little honey to my hair.

There was just a little hair color left after my Mom finished with my Grandmother's hair, so Operation Honey Blonde was in full effect. My mission: to get my hands on that box! I snuck and went into the kitchen, found the left over color, and applied it to my bangs and my then tail (I'm really dating myself, but a tail is a long piece of hair worn in the back of your hairstyle that looks like, well, a tail!)

Afterwards, I acted as if I had some kind of invisible field, as if they wouldn't noticed that my hair was visibly a different color. What I loved was that both my Mother and Grandmother said, "Wow, that really looks nice, Brandi". What would follow would be a slew of beauty explorations including piercing my own ears, giving myself a Salt n' Pepa inspired haircut in college, and my signature ponytail updo – a style that became so popular in my dorm room, its earnings paid for all my expenses that semester.

Your hair is one of, if not the most, transformational tools when it comes to your visual brand. The total look of your hair is somewhat of a symphony with the style, cut, color, care and condition being the instrumentation. When done properly, they produce an asset to your look that can create "signature" status. However, if just one of components are off, it can spell disaster. If you have a really great haircut with a brassy hair color; sadly it nullifies the look of the haircut. Likewise a precision haircut that lacks pizazz suddenly comes to life with the right color and hi-lights. Color can also bring warmth to the complexion of the wearer, as well as dictate the personality of your role.

Remember when we talk about your role's look, we are creating a total package, and part of that package is making sure that every component of your image walks in tandem with the other. So your look can not be complete if you have a great outfit on, manicured nails, great makeup and jacked up hair – it's a fail.

Don't get me wrong; in terms of change, there will be exceptions to the rules. There are some hairstyles that remain timeless, and once you find it, you know you found your signature style. For example, you may be someone who arrives at a uncomplicated style and stays there for years. The bob cut, that never really dates, can easily be up-leveled every season by changing the color, adding precision lines, or a razor cut for texture to make the look current. If the bob fits the wearer and their role, they may have found something that works for them indefinitely or through multiple stages of their lives.

Just as we have taken a look on how to cater your wardrobe to your role, you should now reevaluate all components of your hair to make sure that it's a fit too.

Finding the perfect hairstyle for your role consist of several factors:

Your Lifestyle – Do you work out often and need both fashion and flexibility? Do you travel a lot? Are you photographed or in an arena where you are highly visible which means you have to stay razor sharp? Your lifestyle will be a major factor in your hairstyle of choice.

Maintenance – What will be required to keep the hairstyle in tiptop shape; the color always refreshed, the haircut trimmed, or the extensions installed? You have to calculate the financial investment involved and if you are willing or able to commit to the costs of keeping the hairstyle.

The Shape of your face – Creating a hairstyle that is as flattering to the shape of your face accentuates the positive, and balances elsewhere.

The Texture of your hair- Make sure that you don't have an expectation of a hairstyle that your current texture cannot fulfill, instead choose a hairstyle that works with your hair texture, opt for extensions to increase volume, or treatments to get the effect that will be most flattering and manageable.

Manageability – Is this a hairstyle and/or color that you can keep up at home and in between visits, do you need to explore other options such as extensions? How well can you manage the hairstyle without your stylist?

The 3 C's: Cut, Color, and Care

Cut

You'll know you got a great cut when...

You and the stylist are on the same page. Communication is the key in getting the haircut you desire, and it starts off without one shear in site, but with the initial consultation. If you are unclear about what you want from the beginning, you can't expect the stylist to be able to read your mind. If you feel the need to be in control of the process- you may end up disappointed without having a clear vision yourself. If however you trust the expertise of the hairstylist then allow them the freedom of advising you on what they see for you. But again the key is giving them some ideas to work with such as showing them pics on your visual storyboard of hairstyles you like. Photographs, both of what you do and don't like, will help the stylist visualize your goals – even if you're not completely sure of what you want. Also, a good hairstylist should use your hair texture and face shape to make recommendations. If the stylist rushes the process, does not consider the fore mentioned things, or you're uncomfortable with anything during the consultation – now's the time to speak up, not after you're dissatisfied! The best haircut happens when the client and the stylist work together as a team and it's built on a communicated vision, trust, and respect for the gift of the stylist and you as a valuable client.

You can re-create it at home. The true test of a good haircut isn't how it looks when you leave the salon, it's how well it works for you when you get home and lived a little. You should be able to style your hair yourself, and get a similar look of when you left the salon. If the cut has been manipulated to look good in the salon with styling aids and goes flat when you try to do it yourself, it usually hasn't been cut well. If the cut is simply too hard to maintain at home, it's probably not for you either.

It has some element of versatility. A good haircut will work with your hair's texture, not against it. So if you choose to wet your hair and wear it curly or wear it straight, it should look great either way.

Your friends compliment how good your hair looks, not just the haircut itself. The haircut should be an intricate part in the symphony. When music plays there is one beautiful harmonious melody, not one instrument sticking out tremendously over the other. You want people to see your hair and say "wow that looks great, it's perfect for you".

Color

Strategic hair coloring can...

Enhances any cut. Turn a good haircut into an amazing one by choosing a color that complements your style.

Plays up your features. Strategically placed hair color—like makeup—can help to enhance your features that may have been hidden under a shade less flattering.

Make hair appear super-shiny. If your strands are dry or frizzy looking, consider a color glaze that is guaranteed to boost the look of your hair while adding a luminous shine.

Care

A critical mistake that women make is not being realistic about the time required to maintain the style. They may keep up with their hair for a week then the time commitment seems like too much, and they become disappointed with the results. The best thing to do is talk honestly with the stylist about what it will take to manage your hair, and then commit to playing your part in keeping your hair healthy. It doesn't matter how awesome the haircut and color is if it becomes damaged. If you decide to alternate your visits to the salon, invest in the products needed to keep your hair in tiptop shape, which your stylist can recommend. Clear a definite time and space to condition your hair, and incorporate any daily maintenance with your morning or bedtime routine. Trust me, your hair will thank you.

Day 30

Makeup 101:
Paint Me Polished

I started wearing makeup at age 13. My makeup regimen consisted of 2 items: I wore electric blue eyeliner which doubled as a lip liner used to blend with my Wet n Wild fuchsia lipstick – And that was it. I remember being so proud of having freshly and intricately applied my makeup, only to go out on the porch to see my friend and them say, "You look like a clown!" It's funny now, but back then I thought I did a good job – it was like oh well, back to the drawing board! Who knew that I would grow up to actually get paid by very well known people to paint their faces. It shows that everyone can learn when they apply themselves and get the right formula.

I did not grow up being a glamour queen. In fact, when I look at my wedding pictures I only wore lipstick (still fuchsia!) and eyeliner, but I had fabulous hair.

I had my eyebrows arched for the first time in my junior year of college, and after seeing how different I looked, I immediately went back to my Mom and asked how she could let me spend 20 years of my life with a uni-brow.

I learned the art of makeup because I wanted to offer more in film and television and be more marketable, so I started at Sephora as an artist, moved to MAC, took classes, and the rest came through being self taught.

My grandmother however was a makeup queen. My grandmother was of Sicilian, Indian, and African American descent, and because her skin was olive, had a very hard time finding foundation. In fact, I could say I got some of my makeup skills from her, because she was the official makeup artist for her sisters as each of them had a different beautiful hue of golden brown skin. My Grandmother would take various foundations and pigments and make the perfect shades of foundation for each of my Aunts. When she finished, they all looked like they could walk the red carpet. She loved makeup, and was never caught without a fresh face.

My Grandmother and Mom's method of touching up in the middle of the day was to pinch their cheeks and lips to make a natural flush, a thing that we makeup artist now try to do with products as a faux version of Grandma's technique.

I often find women have 4 different views when it comes to makeup:

1. They don't want to look "made up", so they wear nothing
2. It's too hard to do, so they just wear lipstick, and call it a day
3. They apply too much for everyday wear, (Broadway here I come)
4. They apply the makeup, but by mid day it is non-existent

The 5 Keys to Makeup

1. **Prepare and take care of the skin** – The skin is the foundation of all great makeup application, the better you care for it and prep it, the easier the application will be. i.e. water, skincare, primer, age preventative products

2. **Have the correct tools** – In order to get the right effect and make your job easier, you need the right tools to apply your makeup. Tools = Brushes

3. **The right texture, color, and type of makeup is key** – Choosing flattering colors, and textures of the makeup you use is integral to the results you get. There is not a one size fits all to makeup. You build your signature look, and let it be the foundation of everything else.

4. **Apply in the right places** – This boils down to technique. Knowing how to open up your eye as opposed to making it look droopy, knowing how to sculpt your face so it is defined without looking like a cartoon character. Basically understanding your face and looking

at it as a canvas with many parts that comes together to make a masterpiece.

Natural look and long lasting – One of the biggest frustrations I hear from women is that their makeup doesn't last. When I put on my makeup in the morning, I never touch it again, because I layer the makeup in such a way that it lasts, yet still looks natural. Below I will show you how!

Beauty Essentials
Basic skincare
Cleanser
Facial exfoliator
Moisturizers
Eye cream
Serum
Cold cream
Sunscreen
Anti-aging masks and or treatments, age appropriate

Must-Have Makeup
Primer
Concealer
2 foundations (one for winter, one for summer)
Facial powder
2 blushes
Bronzer
Brow powder
Brow gel
Eyeliner (I love gel liners)
Eyeshadow color palette with light and dark shades and highlighter
Mascara
4 lipsticks (two for winter, two for summer, matte and creamy textures)
An arsenal of lip gloss (my favorite)

Eyelash curler
Tweezers
Set of quality makeup brushes
Anti-shine/blot powder or matte oil blotting papers

8 Makeup Brushes

Foundation
Concealer
Large Powder Brush
Blush Brush
Eyeshadow
Crease Eyeshadow brush
Eyeliner
Brow Angled Firm Brush

Brandi's 10 Step Polished Makeup Formula

Step One: Skincare

Skincare is essential for skin that looks and feels its best. Diet, weather, and stress can affect skin on a daily basis, so adjust your skincare routine accordingly.

Moisturizer gives skin a fresh look and creates the perfect base for makeup. For a flawless smooth application, be sure to apply the primer after your moisturizer.

Step Two: Concealer

The purpose of concealing is to lighten the dark or red areas on the face, and make the skin all one color and even. For under-eye circles start with a corrector to cut through the darkness under the eye.

Next, use Concealer one shade lighter than your complexion to brighten the under-eye area.

There are two ways to apply:

1. Using the Concealer Brush, apply Concealer as close as possible to the lash line, and on the innermost corner of the eye. Gently pat the concealer with your fingers to blend it in.
2. Way to apply Concealer: with clean fingers, usually the middle finger.

Step Three: Foundation

Use your Foundation Brush to apply and blend foundation. Use brisk even strokes starting by dabbing foundation on four points of your face.

Step Four: Powder

For crease-free wear, apply Loose Powder over concealer using an Eye shadow brush, Crease Brush or Powder Puff.

If you have an oily t-zone, apply powder to the rest of your face using a Powder Puff or Powder Brush.

EXTRA TOUCH: To add a warm tint to skin, dust Bronzing Powder over cheeks, using a separate Powder Brush.

Step Five: Brow

Use the clear brow gel to comb brows into shape. For the most natural look, define brows with Eye Shadow that matches your hair color; use the Angled Brush to apply shadow. Begin at the inner corner of the brow and follow its natural shape using light, feathery strokes.

Step Six: Eyeshadow

Sweep a neutral color Eye Shadow color from lash line to crease of eye using the Eye Shadow Brush.

For added definition, dust a deeper Eye Shadow color in the crease, using the Eye Shadow Crease Brush.

Step Seven: Eyeliner

Line the upper lash line with Gel Eyeliner and the Eyeliner Brush. Remember to dab the excess liner off into the cap of the product, and to use what's left (after applying liner to both eyes), to the bottom lashes.

If you also line the lower lash line, make sure top and bottom liner meet at the outer corner of the eye.

Step Eight: Blush

Smile and dust Blush from the sides of your checks to the apples of cheeks with the Blush Brush. Blend up towards the hairline, then downwards to soften color.

Layer a pop of bright blush (applied just on the apples of cheeks) over the neutral shade for a longer lasting look.

If you see a line across your cheeks, use the loose powder and powder brush to buff the line away.

Step Nine: Lips/Liner/Lipstick/Gloss

For natural-looking definition and to keep color from feathering, line lips with Lip Liner after applying lip color. Use the Lip Brush to soften and blend any hard edges.

Next, Use the natural coloring of your lips as a guide when choosing your every – day Lipstick shade. The most flattering shade will either match or be slightly darker than your lips.

Add a small pop of gloss to the center of your lip.

Step Ten: Mascara

Black Mascara makes eyelashes that pop. When applying mascara, brush from base of lashes to tips while rolling the wand to separate lashes and avoid clumps.

If you choose to curl lashes, be sure to do this before applying mascara; curling lashes after mascara makes them more prone to breakage.

Day 31

The Art of Living in Maintain: Learning To Stick and Stay With Your Visual Brand

Maintain: To support a style of living, to keep in an existing state; preserve or retain; to declare to be true

Research shows that it takes 21 days to break or develop a habit or routine.

That's 21 days of going to the gym every day or exercising in some way every day, 21 days to increase your spiritual life, 21 days to eat healthily, 21 days of keeping your house organized. The reality is that when you do a routine long enough, it becomes habit forming both good and bad, because we are creatures of habit. Therefore to break a habit you have to replace it with another action or mindset, and focus on what you want to achieve. The good habit then graduates to becoming *a lifestyle.*

Below I have compiled a cheat sheet to help trigger things that you can do to make life easier and help you maintain your visual brand (and sanity!)

Think about maintaining your look and creating routines for your life from the perspective of "if I stay ready I won't have to get ready".

- Set yourself up to win by preparing to create and maintain a life you love
- By preparing you avoid the frustration that comes with rushing to get things done
- When you maintain you don't have to spend extra time doing the crash course version of the task that could have been done without the extra drama. Drama that inevitably throws you into overwhelm

Maintaining, though challenging in the beginning, becomes the easier route when mastered and applied.

When scheduling your daily routines, rename them something fabulous and rewarding like:

- Exercise: "Snatching My Sexy Back"
- Getting dressed and groomed: "My Red Carpet Routine"

- Eating: "Fueling My Body"
- Prayer: "Communing with God", "Spiritual Refreshment" or "Filling my Spiritual Tank"
- Taking off Makeup or Skin Care Regimen: "Nourishing My Skin"
- Family Time/Date Night: "Loving on my Family", "Keeping My Marriage Spicey!", if single "Building and Exploring Meaningful Relationships"

Maintaining Your Image

- Replace foundation –2 times annually, but this may increase if you have two shades of foundation (one for warmer months, and one for colder months)
- Add on to your makeup kit and regimen seasonally (new seasonal eye shadow, blush, bronzer, mascara, lipgloss)
- Buy 2-3 of everything as it pertains to your makeup, that way you can have one set of makeup that stays home, one that can stay at the office or go with you to work if need be, and one that can always be ready for travel
- Quick Hair Guide
  - Schedule Haircuts:
    - Short hair: 4-5 weeks
    - Medium hair: 4-6 weeks
    - Long hair: 6-8 weeks
    - Schedule Coloring: Every 4-8 weeks
    - Schedule Deep Conditioning Treatment: Every 1- 2 weeks
- Set appointments in advance for eyebrow shaping
- Set appointments in advance for manicures or explore gel manicures that last longer without chipping.
- Look at your work related events, and begin planning your wardrobe shopping around your events ahead of time
- Stage your clothing to be ready to go at a moments notice by

having at least 5 complete outfits on a hanger complete with accessories, and dry cleaned

- Create a budget to buy core items each quarter/season for your wardrobe
- Plan to thoroughly purge your closet every 6 months
- Schedule promotional shoots for new marketing materials annually

Maintain Your Body

- Give yourself a cheat meal each week, but base it off of how well you've eating all week (if you have been eating junky all week, you don't get a cheat meal)
- Set up a strategy plan for high calorie months – meaning a refocusing diet to go on afterward the holidays or major life event or extra cardio before hand to combat enjoying the holidays/event
- Keep healthy snacks in your purse, in your car, at the office, and in your home
- Set quarterly times to detox and clean out your body
- Plan your workouts – period, and sanction that time for yourself to move your body

Maintain Balance with Work/Family Dynamic

- Take a look at your year and schedule projects and tasks in 90 day chunks
- Schedule family time and vacations for the year.
- Consider cooking all of your meals on one day over the weekend, label and put each meal in freezer bags. Then you can take them out the night before the next days dinner. By doing this you are not cooking every day.
- Create the ultimate shopping list with items you always know you will need, along with 5 meals that always work for you

and your family. By knowing the meals you will cook for the week and having one list with all your ingredients, you ease the stress of having to go to the grocery store multiple times a week (which wastes time in the long run).

- If you travel often, keep a ready packed toiletries bag and accessories, that way you never have to prepare you can simply drop in your suitcase
- Plan to have at least one educational/motivational/spiritual enrichment class per quarter/every 90 days
- Get away by yourself to refocus and gain perspective at least once per quarter/90 days
- Review your visual storyboard daily and revisit it's structure every 90 days

And, don't forget to celebrate yourself and your commitment to living in maintain.

The emotion of celebration solidifies and associates pleasurable thoughts with each act of consistency. So when you do your habits and routines enough times your brain starts feeling accomplished. The result is that you then unconsciously want to continue experiencing the feel good emotions that come from knowing you stayed the course.

So, stay the course and master the art of living in maintain!

Day 32

Get On The A-List:
The Power Of A Great
Promotional Headshot

Every actor seeking work has a great headshot. A headshot is a photograph used by actors and actresses in order to get them work. Having a current headshot is a top priority for an actor. It is your calling card and the first step in the casting process.

The actor is very careful to create headshots and other pictures that compliment and clearly show them as the types of roles in which they want to be cast. A great headshot is instrumental in generating new opportunities.

I take this same approach when creating promotional shots with my visual branding clients. While some people in business see a promotional shot as just a picture to attach to their website or bio, I look at it as an opportunity to get you cast in your roles in life.

The power of great headshots and promotional pictures for the artist/ actor:

- Sells for them
- Sells them in the role they want
- Portrays you the way you want to be seen; and can immediately elevate your positioning

Where we use great pictures

- Website
- Info products
- Products
- Book Covers
- Advertising
- Speakers sheet
- Social media profiles
- Bios
- Press kits
- Business cards

- Email signature
- Marketing Materials

Here are some things to keep in mind when planning to take your promotional pictures

Know specifically what you want those pictures to do for you and where they will be seen. Before taking any pictures, you should clearly think out every way you will need to use them. Think about the effect you want them to have, and the various ways they will be seen. If you are not clear in this area you will be shooting in the dark. You can also consult with someone to be clearer about what your goals are and what you will need. Pull pictures where you like looks or advertising to give the photographer and idea of the direction in which you wish to go.

Understand that a great photo takes a team to produce. Besides have a photographer that can capture your true essence, great photography is not complete without the right hair, makeup, and wardrobe.

The Right Photographer. The photographer should be one who has done the caliber of work you expect, it should be visible on their website and marketing tools. The most important thing is that you are comfortable with the photographer. Referrals from a colleague are great as well. You want someone with experience. You want someone you get along with and will be able to communicate with freely. The photographer should also be able to be very good with lighting, and have the skills to do retouching. If they do not retouch themselves, they should have a third party that they use to provide a finished product.

Makeup & Hair. The truth is that cameras pick up everything. If your foundation is uneven, if your eye shadow has a sharp line, if you have hair that looks flat, or pieces out of place, it will show up on your pictures. Having a professional makeup and hair stylist helps you to have a great picture because not only do they do the service for you, but if you have one or both at the shoot with you, they usually have a meticulous eye to make sure you are perfect frame by frame. And although you want pictures that aren't overly or under done, you have to have the balance of having enough make up on to show up in the pictures, but applied in a way that you still look like yourself. There is a reason why make-up and hairstylist are used on every set, it's because they are a necessary part of the team to turn out a wonderful picture. So, don't skimp on your headshots by cutting out the make-up and hair artists.

Picking out wardrobe. The wardrobe that you wear should tie in specifically to your role and the way you want to be seen. The key is less is more, simple, clean lines, and light on the patterns. Solid colors work best, and if you have a signature color in your marketing you can incorporate it into your clothing. It is very important that your clothing fits well and has a tailored look, if not, it will likely add extra pounds that you may not want (besides the camera adds weight any way). You should bring at least 3 changes of clothing, but have a couple of spare choices just in case. Cameras will pick up wrinkles, so make sure that all clothing is pressed well.

How Often Do I Need To Get Headshots Done?

Most people who are marketing themselves should get fresh shots every year. In my experience the people who take new shots annually are continually moving forward in their roles, and therefore are evolving in their promotional pictures. Their shots get better and better because they are getting to the place of owning who they are and what they do and it shows in their pictures.

Let these questions help you decide when it's time for new pictures:

- You have used the pictures so much, you are tired of them
- You look very different than the pictures (you may have lost weight/ gained weight, have different hair, or aged)

- The picture doesn't fit the tone of your role any longer or you've changed directions in your role
- You seek to change the perception of your role or up-level your positioning.
- The picture feels dated

Day 33

Receiving the Callback: Look the Part in Your Marketing Materials

Callback: An invitation to return for a second audition or interview

How to Look The Part in With Your Marketing Materials

By now I think you get the point that you never get a second chance to make a first impression. This is certainly true with your company's marketing materials. A new client often takes many pieces of information away from their first glimpse of a marketing piece or website. And this impression can make the difference between whether they choose to want to know more about you and read on or decide to recycle with your materials.

LOOK THE PART TO GET THE ROLE extends to your marketing pieces; you want to assure that what you put in that person's hand actually grabs their interest and prompts them to want to learn more, do business with you either now or in the future, consider your proposal, or buy your product.

Good Marketing Materials should:

- Impress on first glance
- Directly tell what you do
- Be presented with high quality materials, i.e. quality of paper, vibrant colors, and clear legible text
- Compliment each other, match visually (same color scheme, fonts), and contain the same messaging which should be compatible with all of your pieces

Traditional marketing pieces are:

1. Business cards
2. Brochure
3. Postcards
4. Press kit
5. Speaker's sheet
6. Menu of Services

7. Proposals
8. Letterhead
9. Posters
10. Banners
11. Logos

Before they start reading the text, review your figures, or look at your logo, your potential client will first get an overall feel of what you represent from the marketing piece you just gave them.

Here are 5 elements that will guide your potential client:

1. Incorporating a color palette. How well your color choices are on-message for your visual brand and appropriate for your target market. Once you have a definite group of colors and fonts you use in your visual brand, you will want to incorporate them all of the time.

2. How and where your colors land on the page. Do the colors flow through the marketing piece? Is one color dominant, with highlights of a secondary color? When you understand the effect color placement has on your marketing piece, you will begin to look at it as another form of communication. Your color sets a mood.

3. The layout of the elements in the piece. The clients' eyes need to land exactly where you want them to on your piece at first glance. Usually it's best if their eyes scroll down as opposed to side to side. You want to make it easy for them to read. You will also need to observe the overall arrangement of information and graphics on the page.

4. The photos. When you include a photo in your marketing materials, your viewers immediately equate the value of what you do with how the pictures look. If the pictures are unprofessional or dated, you are sending a message that your services may be also.

5. The white space. White space is the empty spaces in a design. White space is used to separate design elements and group similar ones. White space is not always "white" — it is the empty parts of the page, but if the page has a different background color that will be the color of the white space. White space can make a design feel free and open. It also gives viewers' eyes a place to rest while taking in design and text.

**How you can examine your material to see
if it's telling the story you want:**

1. Get feedback from clients or people that would fit your idea client's profile. Your goal is to get their first impression, and not allow too much time for them to sit and ponder. If you give them too much time they will over analyze the piece and go into process mode. You want an immediate impression of your piece – so give them a short window of time say 5 minutes (you can call them and simultaneously send the email for them to look at with you via phone) or get immediate feedback in person to truly know what they think.

2. Perform your own glance test. Take your marketing piece, print it, put it on a table, leave the room, and go look at something else for a few minutes. If you're working on a website, email newsletter, blog, or some other online design piece, pull it up on your monitor and take a screen shot of it to print.

Go on with your day, then, go back and look at it with fresh eyes as if you've never seen it before. What do you think?

3. Measure your piece according to the above 5 elements I've mentioned. Really look at your piece with a meticulous eye. Does it match your role, and your message? What about congruency in the layout, color palette, white space, and what about the strength of your photos? Think about each of these elements in the context of the message that you want your role to convey.

4. Gather some comparison materials. Your customers will likely receive your materials at a networking event, trade show, conference, by mail, or online. So you'll want to know how your materials rate in comparison to the other materials they'll be gathering collectively. The easiest way to do this is by collecting these items yourself during those same kinds of events. Once you gather some materials, lay them out and put yours side by side with them. Make a checklist of what you like and what you don't like, and then how you can improve.

When up-leveling your marketing pieces, here are things to consider to take your pieces from meeting the recycle bin to being memorable enough they post it on their wall to keep:

Use your messaging by writing effective headlines. The point of a headline is to catch people's attention and give them a reason to keep reading. On point ones have selling power. In addition, if you have a slogan, or tagline phrase that embodies what you do, use it creatively on your materials.

Make a consistent and cohesive presentation. Organize your piece by first creating an outline from which to work. This should include your messaging, what you want to convey, and consistent key words you want to always used associated with your visual brand (i.e. mines is be polished, packaged, and promoted), product or services, contact info, and marketing message. Don't let inconsistencies in your message and organization distract readers and dilute what you have to say.

Keep it simple when writing. Readers are in a hurry. Get to your point the easiest and most concise way possible.

Use my P.E.T.S formula – *Lay out the PROBLEM, use EMOTIONAL TRIGGERS, then offer a SOLUTION.*

- **Show me... me.** Readers care only about how the information presented affects their own lives. How can you solve their problems? Do they know they have a problem? Address your readers' needs and desires, and explain how your services will help them.

- **Use emotional triggers.** Which worries and desires keep them up at night? What are the benefits they hope to attain by using your services? What are the key words and phrases that ignite a "oh, that's me" response?

- **Offer a Solution.** To sell through words, you need to identify and appeal to your readers' needs and then offer them a solution. Making your readers feel understood makes them more likely to trust that the solution you're offering will work for them. What are the results you deliver?

Look at what your competitors have done. Research your competitors' marketing materials and analyze the strengths and weaknesses. How can you make your product improve on your findings? What can you offer to enhance what's already out there? *Note: This is not about competition, it is a part of research and development. When you truly understand who you are and what you have to offer, you will find that the only competition is you.*

Day 34

Make Them Cast You
Upon First Click!
Look the Part Online

Looking the Part Online – Achieving love at first click

Two of the most beneficial tools you will have to convey your message is your website and the ability to bring connectivity to your audience through video. In fact, I saw my business completely revolutionize through video marketing and having a website that served as my 24 hour store. Having a well designed web site will not only be beneficial to your business in today's electronic world but will also help you save money.

Great websites increase your reach and availability through having a 24 /7 operation. Your website works for you while you sleep; generating new leads, earning revenue, and making introduction to what you do to visitors across the globe. Not only will your website be there 24 hours a day, 365 days a year with the possibility of reaching millions of people every day, but now even when your office doors close, your site still is able to service clients. For some it is their primary way of doing business, and many people are doing quite well financially completely virtual. That's why you have to invest the time and energy in building one that will benefit you and be operational to do exactly what you like.

Great websites immediately allow you to market to your audience, thereby saving advertising costs. I love the fact that you can create a new product or get a speaking date and within 5 minutes all of the information is available and in your virtual store online. It's simply amazing to me. The Internet has leveraged the playing ground for many entrepreneurs, authors, and businesses that would not be able to afford marketing through traditional methods. The freedom of being able to change the content on your site without having to ask someone to do it for you is extremely liberating and cost effective.

Great websites provide one central place to showcase your products/ services. A website provides the immediate opportunity to communicate to the public all of who you are and why someone can work with you. It puts all of your services and offering in one neat tidy place for people to make an educated decision. It also allows the customer to take the time to get to know you as well before they work with you; something that may be difficult to do if you are in New York and your client is in Tokyo.

Great websites allow interactive communication leading to greater marketing. It used to be that a website read as a brochure, one that people visited one time and never returned because there was no reason for them to revisit. Today you can have an ongoing conversation with your audience by implementing blogs on your site as well as them subscribing to the things you say on other media platforms.

Great websites provide a platform to do market research Great marketing definitely includes market research and receiving feedback from your customers. You can use features on your website such as surveys, polls, and track your website statistics to find out exactly what your customers want and then narrow your focus to what they want.

Great websites are designed to be an extreme marketing machine for you. It's not about bells and whistles, it's about communicating with your audience and quickly bringing them to a decision to want to work with you.

10 Ways to Look Like a Pro When
Marketing Yourself Through Online Videos

1. Be yourself, enjoy making the video, and have fun with it!
If you are uncomfortable and not enjoying making your video, this will be magnified dramatically on screen. Don't make your video if you are in a bad mood. Wait until you are in a good mood and feeling happy and passionate about your subject matter. Don't forget to smile often. This will also have an effect on how viewers engage with you and how long they will watch your video for.

2. Know what you are going to say
Don't waste your own time by sitting in front of a camera and just making

up your entire script as you go along. This doesn't necessarily mean your video needs to be scripted – there are advantages to the qualities you can create with spontaneity. However it will help to have some bullet points so that you ensure you don't miss anything out. Knowing your general structure in advance will also help you to create a much better quality video.

3. Be aware of your lighting and make sure it's flattering
Be aware of the light in the room when you are filming. Shooting during the day is always an advantage as you can make the most of the natural light through your windows. Also, think about the directions your lights are coming from and the shadows they create on your face and in your surroundings. Another option is to shoot your video where there are no windows, that way you can control all the light with the lights you provide.

4. Dress the part of your role, as if you were meeting your viewers in person
Just because you are filming yourself at home is not an excuse to not look the part. Dress as you would if meeting with your audience in person. Give extra consideration to how it looks on screen, including the colors in the background. Being against a white background is a big mistake and won't do anything for your skin tone. Wear colors that will make you stand out and compliment your face. If you are unsure, take some test shots in different outfits and look at them on different devices so you can see what works and what doesn't.

5. Frame your shot by thinking about what to put in it
Consider what is in the background and where you will place yourself in relation to what is there. Always off center yourself to be more pleasing to the viewer. Think about the angle of the camera and your eye level. The camera should be level with your eyes.

6. Look into the lens so that you are making 'eye contact' and connect with your viewers
If you are making a video in which you are meant to be speaking directly

to your audience, look into the lens of your camera. If you are not looking at the audience and looking somewhere else, you will hinder the audiences' ability to connect with you and what you are saying.

7. Engage your audience through inflection in your voice, and being conversational

Have energy when you speak, but don't be too fast or salesy. Getting your pace right will make a massive difference to how long viewers will watch your video.

8 Know your audience and speak their language

Speak your audiences' language: keywords, phrases, etc. Your audience needs to know that you're both on the same page as them. Keep it short and simple.

9. Speak in easily digestible sound bites – no run on sentences. I got this advice straight from someone I admire a great deal Iyanla Vanzant. She personally coached me on how to speak in short sound bites thereby making what I said impactful and empowering. From that point on, I started being especially aware of every word and syllable I spoke, making sure that it counted, and had a start point and an easy stop point as if it were being edited.

10. Develop a tagline you use during your intro and when finishing the video for branding and consistency

Other places where your visual brand should be consistent online are:

Social media sites and their branding:

- Facebook cover design, and profile pictures
- Twitter background
- You tube background

Day 35
Is That the Same Person?
Look the Part By
Being Consistent In
Person and Online

Continuity: The state or quality
of being continuous.

The Necessity of Continuity in Your Look

On the set it is the responsibility of the script supervisor to see that continuity is maintained between takes and between the setups. This means that the actors must be wearing the same clothes, the same jewelry, and the same hairstyle. If a candle or cigarette is half burned down in one take then it must be the same in all takes.

Without visual continuity a movie becomes a series of unnatural jarring moments that take the audience out of the illusion that your movie is a depiction of real life.

When everything in the shot, scene and movie is consistent, then you've succeeded in maintaining continuity.

And the same goes for the continuity between your marketing materials, online, and offline presence. You should be able to create a continuous uninterrupted story through your visual brand that remains consistent no matter in what medium someone meets you.

Once you have created the blueprint for your visual brand – it doesn't stop there. Now you must maintain your look and strive to live in continuity in your own story. You have to decide that you will keep up your look on a day-to-day basis when in the public.

Nothing is more disarming than when someone hands you a polished business card with a beautiful picture on the front, and you literally can't recognize that it's the same person. You are thinking are you their representative? The picture is either many years old, or the person simply doesn't put forth any semblance of an effort to duplicate the look they have chosen to brand themselves.

It becomes very difficult to become recognizable both online and off when you don't try to duplicate some version of the polished look you present on your marketing materials.

In film and television actors are chosen for parts based on their headshots, because the headshot allows the decision maker to find their character esthetically and cast them as the role. If that same actor shows up to the audition looking different than their pictures, they could very well lose their opportunity to have the role because they are not representing the image they projected on their headshot.

How to have continuity in your look from your pictures to in person contact

1. **Develop a uniform in your wardrobe.** Once you have your core wardrobe in place, you will find that you have particular combinations of clothing that you gravitate towards. Your uniform therefore might be a colored sheath dress and colorful heels when presenting on stage and a business casual look of jeans, a white button up shirt, and blazer when meeting with friends. The more you find combinations that work in your various life environments you will see that you have a type of uniform that works in your life's events.

2. **Maintain the hairstyle in your marketing materials for at least a year so that the pictures you present will be consistent with the pictures you display in your marketing materials**

3. **Ask your hairstylist to give you a tutorial on how to maintain your hairstyle for everyday wear and special events.** You can buy the tools and hair supplies that will allow you to most represent your hairstyle in the best light possible, and do so with ease.

4. **Develop a signature makeup palette filled with 3-6 makeup colors you can wear in a particular color family.** Invest the time and

effort in knowing how to do your makeup for events so that even if it does not look like you've been touched by a professional makeup artist, you are at least in the ballpark.

5. **When you go to various events take pictures of yourself each time and create a look book of your various looks.** Determine what worked well and do more of it consistently. For example, if your hair looks really good with more body and parted on the side, and not so good with curls, recalling the pictures will allow you to see first hand what looks good and what does not.

6. **Consistency simply builds visual brands.** Stick with your brand. Once you have established an authentic and polished look don't try to change your visual brand image unless you're certain that it's no longer appropriate for the market. Clarity and consistency are key to getting it right – each and every time!

Day 36

Do They Represent You?
Look the Part Through
Your Supporting Cast

How's Your Supporting Cast?

I am sure you have made every effort to hire and contract the best individuals for your company, but how do others perceive them? Are you confident that your employee's actions, attitudes, dress, and communication skills really "sell" your visual brand to the public and others in your industry?

Your company image is talking, even when your staff is not. Therefore when your team looks good, you look good! With just a little guidance from you, each and every person that represents you can "sell" your brand by presenting a polished, highly relatable version of who you are and become an extension of what you want to express to the world.

Why is this so important?

They are your brand ambassadors. They represent your brand and are a reflection of you that demonstrates your businesses culture through their look, vibe, display of integrity and demeanor.

Perception Management. When done correctly, their image presence creates a level of trust in your business and brand through consistency and uniformity.

Improved morale and boost of confidence to your employee or contractor. When your employee looks good and feels good they will be more confident to perform better for your business.

How to Communicate Your Visual Brand Through Your Supporting Cast to Boost Your Company Image

#1 Lead by example. You will set the standard for those who work with you. You cannot ask from them what you are not willing to do for your own image; you could, but it may seem hypocritical. When you present a consistent look and feel of how you want to do business, people will usually adapt to the pulse of what you establish *and* maintain.

#2 Create the culture and model for your company image. Image should reflect the culture of the business as well as personal style. Inappropriate clothes or grooming can invalidate the individual and even the entire department or business. An inappropriate image creates a barrier to immediate communication and may create a negative first impression.

#3 Provide global etiquette examples. With the exception of marketing materials and your online presence, your employees and contractors may be the first point of contact for your customers and clients. No matter the geographical location, those that represent you should adapt to the expected behaviors, attire, and company image.

#4 Write policies. There are some employees and contractors who simply won't know how to observe the dress culture, so it is better to simply put in place a standard of what you expect so there will be no confusion. Provide clear dress guidelines in your business and be ready and willing to provide consequences to those that do not follow the policy.

#5 Provide professional appearance and etiquette training. Offer employees a professional image seminar if they lack basic know-how in this area and reinforce dress code guidelines during new employee orientation.

It should include:

- **Physical Examples.** Models of dress for your culture

- **Event attire.** How to dress for particular events (i.e. presentations, speaking, networking events, sales, meetings)

- **Define dressing appropriately for your culture.** In a more conservative environment (executive training, accounting, teaching, etc.) dressing "sexy" can be perceived as "provocative," and prevent you from attracting the kind of attention that wins you credibility and respect. Likewise, in a more artsy industry, dressing in an uneventful, conservative suit will cause people to doubt your creativity and ability to relate. Dressing to fit your profession or industry and the situation, goes a long way toward making you feel like you belong with the team and with that particular business culture.

- **Emphasis on dressing consistently.** Dressing appropriately one day and inappropriately the next sends mixed messages causing confusion for the individual and the observer. Make sure that the way your supporting cast dresses remains consistent with both your professional goals and your audience's expectations.

- **Attitude.** Is everybody excited and appear happy about the work they do? Every single member of your staff, no matter what the job description, is a brand ambassador and will be a reflection of what you may be like as the owner. An employee that is unhappy or has a bad attitude, or an attitude that simply doesn't reflect you (i.e. you are very laid back and creative, and the person that represents you is a stick in the mud), can do unfavorable things to your business image.

#6 Set a timeline for refreshers and evolving. Establish a time period for refreshers. Just as your own personal look will evolve, and fashion changes, it will more often than not cause tweaks to your businesses look and feel. Be willing to allow for periodical review of your business image, and allot time and resources for up leveling.

Day 37

Act Like You Already
Won the Gold Statue

The ultimate mark of an actor's career is being celebrated for the work they have done through awards, and of course being recognized by the academy. It says to the winner, whether they choose to admit it or not, "I have arrived, I am one of the best, I know this, and you recognize me as such".

I spent a great time of my career consulting new singers and actors. One of my best pieces of advice to them when developing their look and persona was to look like they already won the Grammy, had the contract, and were a top selling artist. And my reason for that is simple: if you believe yourself to be great, others will too.

If you already look the part of an artist, others will take you seriously and be more likely to listen to what you have to say.

When you already look like you've won, then I want to be apart of what you do; who doesn't want to be with a winner?

Now this doesn't mean that you act diva-like, or as a know-it-all. There has to be balance. It means you have the confidence and look of one who can do that which you say you can do, coupled with the attitude of someone that people want to do business with.

When you act like you have already won, and your demeanor is grounded with self-assurance and self-belief, others will want to buy into your brand.

**How to act like you have already got your role,
but remain inspired while in pursuit**

Whatever you want to do, start doing it now. Every part of your journey counts and is a learning lesson on many levels. Want to be a writer? Start a blog. Want to be a designer? Start making clothes. People that keep talking about what they are going to do usually will still be talking about the same thing, in more detail, in years to come.

Act like you already have the job. Embody the role you want. Begin to dress the way you want to be perceived. When you show up to events, look the part of the role you want. Psych yourself out if need be by creating visual examples of you in your new role; like your company's name in a big ad, or your face as a speaker in a major conference. If it benefits your confidence and inspires you, who cares? No one needs to know you walk around imagining you're on the set everyday but you.

Celebrate every small step. Sometimes we can feel that we are so far from our goals, but remind yourself of what you want, and remain diligent to take the daily, weekly, and monthly actions toward your goal. You need to feel like you're making progress, and allowing yourself to feel great about the small achievements is critical.

Be constantly inspired. Consider every step of your journey a small step on the path to benefit some aspect of your ultimate role. If you're currently a server in a restaurant but aspiring to be a CEO, think of each customer in your restaurant as an opportunity to do market research and provide exceptional customer service to everyone you serve. Instead of hating your job, look at every day as another opportunity to hone your skills.

Do your research. Learn all you can about the role you want through books, the internet, and seminars. Become so familiar with your role before you even start doing it that it will feel like second nature once it's a reality because you have been practicing occupying your role. Staying involved and immersed in your role will provide energy to help you continue moving forward.

Day 38

Use Cue Cards Where Needed. Remind Yourself Of Who You Are To Stay Motivated

Cue cards are cards with words written on them that help actors and speakers remember what they have to say. They are typically used in television production where they can be held off-camera and are unseen by the audience.

When television performers deliver their monologues, they often rely on unseen prompts known as cue cards. These cards are usually made from poster-size card stock, with individual lines and cues written by hand with large markers.

Even if an actor or host is improvising or speaking off-script, cards can provide him or her with the essential information to get back on track.

Sometimes in the midst of living life, we get thrown off our path. In the process, we lose ourselves, and forget our script.

I've been there; I have been at points where I realized that I needed to get back to myself. What did I love? What didn't I love? What is important in my life? It was only after reminding myself of who I was through my own form of cue cards and affirmations that I was able to give fully to the people around me.

Many of my clients use this same cue card technique to stay on track and motivated in their roles. You can create your cue cards with index cards that you can write on and keep with you no matter where you are both at home or in the office.

The cue cards you choose to create can also be used daily as an overall commitment to improve the quality of your life and those who are around you. With each card you cue yourself to remember what's important and be encouraged to stay on track whether it be with your health, embracing your role, asking for help, and maintaining your visual brand.

Your cue cards could include phrases, favorite quotes, and personal affirmations. Some of my cue cards include phrases like:

- "I will have balance in my life"
- "Yes, I do know what I want, but surrender all of my wants and agenda to God to be given back to me with his stamp of approval"

- "I will chose carefully who I share my dreams with, realizing that everyone is not able to see my vision"
- "I will take the time to smell the roses, and dance"
- "I will stay committed to living a healthy life and that means what I eat, consistently moving my body, and having a healthy mindset"
- "I will willfully evolve as my roles begin to evolve"
- "I will remain coachable and focused"
- "I will refer back to my goals and celebrate my accomplishments no matter how small"
- "Me, yes me, I am beautiful at this very moment"

And my most favorite cue card:

- "I take ownership of being fabulous and will not dim my light so that others will feel more comfortable, instead I will lovingly hand them sunglasses"

Day 39

Perfect Practice Makes Perfect Performance: Stay Ready For Your Big Break

Practice does not make perfect.
Only perfect practice makes perfect.
– Vince Lombardi

Right now as you read this, athletes are training, chefs are cooking, speakers are rehearsing, actors are running lines, and dancers are dancing the world over.

Chances are, they're not going through the motions either – they're really doing it. They are practicing "perfectly"; pretending it's the real performance with every rehearsal. That doesn't mean without mistakes, it just means they are putting their all into the practice, and not going through the motions just because it's practice.

That's what they need to do to be the best.

The only way to achieve your roles maximum performance potential is to train your body and mind to do so over and over... and over.

Let's assume for a moment that being good at what you do naturally is not enough. There will always be people who are naturally more talented at certain things than others, just like there will be people who appear to be naturally fit – but no one can achieve great heights without lots and lots of practice and knowing how to fully package what they have.

And your visual brand and role are no exceptions. In order to fully embrace the techniques, tips, and mindset of what I have shared with you over these 40 days it will take practice. You will need to practice building your confidence, practice consistently applying your makeup, practice demonstrating your role, and practice looking the part.

It means practicing like you are performing on every audition to get your roles in life, and being in a constant state of showing up to win every time through your visual brand.

Many people don't know this, but I have been a member of the marching band and symphonic bands since I was 11 years old as a clarinet player.

261

In fact, I credit my tenacity, drive, showmanship, and commitment to excellence to what I learned as being a part of some of the greatest musical institutions in the country. From playing in a great high school band the Mackenzie High School Band of Renown underneath the direction of Bobby L Brown, to practicing and performing in countless halftime shows as a member of the Florida A&M Incomparable Marching 100 under the direction of Dr. William P. Foster and Dr. Julian White.

One of the things that I was taught as a part of the FAMU Marching 100 is that each and every time you practice a performance; you should do so with the level of excellence as if it is the actual performance.

This same philosophy can easily be transferred into business as well; to maximize every opportunity you are afforded as if it were "the one". Your practice and determination to stay ready; to fully demonstrate your role, is just what you need to separate you from the other people auditioning, and advance you to your next level.

Looking at practicing and maintaining your visual brand from this mindset really helps you to be more focused on what it is that you actually want and how you present yourself in the pursuit of your role.

When you practice perfectly, you don't have to ever get ready for your big break – you stay ready.

Day 40

Always Remember to
Thank The Director:
Live a Life of Gratitude,
Appreciation, and Service

When I first started my career in makeup, I remember hearing a great makeup artist, Sam Fine, talk about how he showed his appreciation by sending simple hand written notes saying thank you to his clients and a tube of lipstick. His act of appreciation was something that always stuck with me in business, and one practice I did repeatedly on productions. In fact, on the bottom of my invoices to my production houses, it said "thank you so much for the opportunity to work on producing your vision". I can't tell you how many responses I received reciprocating the thank you. I even got referred to a job because they thought it was so nice that I reached out after the job wrapped to express my gratitude.

Thank you is a powerful statement.

But I am thankful; in so many ways.

I never want to take for granted the opportunities given to me in life to be a co-creator with God; to enjoy this life He has given.

I realize that every job, client, idea, and the beauty of life – everything, deserves my ultimate expression of gratitude to my Director, the Director of my life, God.

How great is it to know there is someone who is in charge, directing and orchestrating every scene of your story, intricately casting every person, location, and plot. He masterfully allows the conflict to make our character stronger, and allows us to emulate Him through our lives. As we go through transitioning from extra, to supporting cast member, to the lead of our lives and roles, I love the fact that in His eyes we are always "the star".

I challenge you, even dare you, to play out your role to the fullest. The most fabulous version of you, the most confident version of you; standing in both power and humility at the same time.

In gratitude, play big in your role, knowing that by you fully owning who you are you are identified to the audience to which you serve.

The true gold of looking the part and getting the role is that in the process you get to communicate in true authenticity and unapologetic boldness who you are, and thereby draw those you are meant to serve. Through visual branding yourself, gaining more confidence, and clearly understanding your role, you make yourself and your message that much clearer, bringing you closer to fulfilling your purpose.

I am also grateful for each one of you; that you choose me to lead you through this forty-day journey to the best and next version of you. I look forward to our paths crossing and seeing you play full out and rocking your role!

Always remember to ......
Know your role.
Play it well,
..... and look fabulous doing it!

ABOUT THE AUTHOR

Brandi Mitchell is founder and director of The Visual Branding Institute, and KORIS Publishing LLC. Brandi is the "secret sauce" that top players in the speaking, corporate, and entrepreneurial arena choose when they are looking to reinvent themselves, polish their presence, and up level their credibility. With skill, care, and ease, she produces stellar images, head-to-toe and photograph to promotion for those seeking to go to the next level of themselves and their business.

But Brandi doesn't just transform her client's image, she teaches them how to maintain the look for themselves and incorporate it in all they do from the stage to a room of few. Brandi Mitchell's proven track record and multi-facted edge of giving her clients a comprehensive wrap around transformation experience comes as a result of her more than 20 years as a celebrity makeup and hair artist, promotional marketing consultant, and art director.

She has worked on projects with some of the world's greatest performers including best selling author, and comedienne Steve Harvey, Oscar Winner Anthony Mackie, Ruby Dee, Eric Benet, Grammy Award Winning Artist, Chrisette Michelle and Eminem, NASCAR driver Kyle Petty and more. She has consulted for LOREAL PARIS, and worked on television shows for TLC, TBS, BET, MTV, and TV ONE. As comfortable in front of the camera as she is behind the lens, Brandi has been an on-air contributor to the Fox Morning Show, Michael Baisden Show, and seen in OPRAH'S O Magazine among others.